BEEF

Edible

Series Editor: Andrew F. Smith

EDIBLE is a revolutionary new series of books dedicated to food and drink that explores the rich history of cuisine. Each book reveals the global history and culture of one type of food or beverage.

Already published

Apple Erika Janik *Beef* Lorna Piatti-Farnell *Bread* William Rubel *Cake* Nicola Humble *Caviar* Nichola Fletcher *Champagne* Becky Sue Epstein *Cheese* Andrew Dalby *Chocolate* Sarah Moss and Alexander Badenoch *Cocktails* Joseph M. Carlin *Curry* Colleen Taylor Sen *Dates* Nawal Nasrallah *Gin* Lesley Jacobs Solmonson *Hamburger* Andrew F. Smith *Herbs* Gary Allen *Hot Dog* Bruce Kraig *Ice Cream* Laura B. Weiss *Lemon* Toby Sonneman *Lobster* Elisabeth Townsend *Milk* Hannah Velten *Offal* Nina Edwards *Olive* Fabrizia Lanza *Oranges* Clarissa Hyman *Pancake* Ken Albala *Pie* Janet Clarkson *Pizza* Carol Helstosky *Pork* Katharine M. Rogers *Potato* Andrew F. Smith *Rum* Richard Foss *Sandwich* Bee Wilson *Soup* Janet Clarkson *Spices* Fred Czarra *Tea* Helen Saberi *Whiskey* Kevin R. Kosar *Wine* Marc Millon

Beef

A Global History

Lorna Piatti-Farnell

REAKTION BOOKS

Published by Reaktion Books Ltd
33 Great Sutton Street
London EC1V 0DX, UK
www.reaktionbooks.co.uk

First published 2013

Printed and bound in China by C&C Offset Printing Co., Ltd

British Library Cataloguing in Publication Data
Piatti-Farnell, Lorna, 1980-
Beef : a global history. – (Edible)
1. Beef 2. Beef industry 3. Cooking (Beef).
I. Title II. Series
641.3´62-DC23

ISBN 978 1 78023 081 8

Contents

I

Of Beef and Cattle

The history of beef is, to some extent, the history of human civilization. Beef – also known as *Bos domesticus* – takes us back to the dawn of human evolution and the consumption of this particular meat has been intertwined with the history of mankind around the world. In prehistoric times, our ancestors were known to have hunted aurochs, a type of wild – and rather ferocious – cattle that were also the ancestor to modern livestock. Now extinct, aurochs bulls are said to have reached a height of 1.8 metres (6 feet), while cows were considerably smaller, reaching only 1.5 metres (5 feet) in height. Cave paintings from several regions in Western Europe depicting detailed hunting scenes testify to the importance of the aurochs to prehistoric *Homo sapiens*, as the meat from these animals represented a large amount of the food rations within hunter-gatherer tribes.

Indeed, it seems virtually impossible to discuss the global history of beef without first talking about cows. This animal has had such an impact on human societies and cultures over millennia, that its ultimate transformation into beef seems hardly a point of departure. The domestication of cattle was not just a matter of food; it also had an impact on human evolution. Many archaeological and anthropological perspectives

...e emphasized different aspects of how cows transformed ...uman existence. Domestication as such occurred in human organizations 12,000 years ago and primarily concerned small animals such as goats, sheep and pigs. Evidence of the domestication of cattle, however, is present from 8000 BC onwards. The Fertile Crescent – encompassing ancient Mesopotamia and now identified with a large area of the Middle East – has often been credited as the place of origin for cattle domestication. Nonetheless, the act in itself, and the consequent consumption of beef that derived from it, has been documented throughout history in a myriad of civilizations. And as far as hunter-gatherer communities were concerned, the domestication of cattle changed things drastically and permanently. Once cows were domesticated, and agriculture flourished as a result, the way of the hunter-gatherer ceased to be. For the most part, humans abandoned their nomadic existence and began to live in organized tribes. Cattle were

Prehistoric depictions of aurochs, from a cave painting in Lascaux, France.

A modern rendition of the prehistoric auroch.

raised for their meat; this was the beginning of what I like to refer to as 'beef' and all that the definition entails.

However, and in spite of the fact that signs of cattle domestication are present independently in the prehistoric histories of several countries around the world, the exact reasons that spurred early humans to approach the vicious wild aurochs are unknown. Indeed, humans are known to have dealt with cattle across the globe, developing their ideas on domestication in completely separate circumstances; the presence and consumption of cattle in prehistory has been documented from the southeastern Sahara in Africa to the Indus Valley (an area now part of modern Pakistan). And yet, in archaeological terms, the reasons behind early attempts at domesticating wild cattle for food, while our ancestors had already ample access to domesticated goats and sheep, are still open to debate.

A likely explanation that has been widely developed in the last two centuries by archaeologists and anthropologists alike seems to have a spiritual foundation at its heart. The

A gift of beef on an ancient Egyptian bas-relief.

attraction that the prehistoric cattle exercised on our early ancestors clearly went beyond their perspective potential as food. In 1896, anthropologist Eduard Hahn already presupposed that, as far as the human relationship with first wild and later domesticated cattle was concerned, the connection was reliant on the symbol of the moon, already an emblem of fertility in 7000 BC. Hahn contended that the distinctively curved shape of the cattle's horn was reminiscent of the moon's nascent crescent, inspiring early humans to associate with the animals on a more permanent basis. In the *Cambridge World History of Food* (2001), Kenneth Kiple and Kriemhild Coneè Ornelas also contend that the wild aurochs were specifically domesticated with religious purposes in mind, as their milk (and later meat) was perceived to be a 'ritual gift from the goddess'. Indeed, the ritualistic and spiritual value of cows remained strong for centuries, if not millennia, as examples of sacred cows and revered oxen – often perceived as incarnations of deities – can be identified in the religious systems of several ancient civilizations and modern nations, ranging from Europe, to Africa and the Middle East. The most prominent example of this is of course India, where Hinduism perceives cows as sacred and, as historian Hannah Velten points out, 'mothers of the Universe', associated as they are with the goddess Prithvi. India has the largest concentrated population of cows in the world; unsurprisingly, however, and in virtue of their religious associations, the slaughter and consumption of cattle is forbidden in most areas of the country. Indeed, the consumption of beef – seen as an abomination by most strands of Hinduism – has formed one of the building blocks for the longstanding rivalry with and dislike of neighbouring Muslim and beef-eating cultural factions, now mainly residing in Pakistan.

By 4000 BC, cattle were fully domesticated and had become a reliable presence in human groups. They had also evolved into two main and distinct sub-categories, which formed the basis for the development of cow species around

Sacred cows in India.

Ancient Egyptian mural depicting both beef and dairy cattle.

the world: these are known as the 'humpless' cattle (*Bos taurus*)
– which developed originally in Africa and the Near East –
and the 'humped' cattle (*B. indicus*), more indigenous to
Indian regions. Velten asserts that, without a doubt, these
two species played an 'enormous role in shaping civilisation',
impacting not only on lifestyle – their culinary uses convert-
ing human existence from nomadic to sedentary – but also
functioning as an important socio-economic expression of
wealth. Cattle were used for work – providing an unparalleled
aid in the development of agriculture – and in the production
of dairy products. Cattle skins also provided warmth against
the elements, transforming the cow into an all-round reliable
source for all human necessities. As distinctions between dairy
cattle and cattle intended for meat consumption evolved over
the centuries, beef became not only a primary source of food
– an obvious and expected development given the size of
cattle and the large amounts of meat they could produce –
but also an important item carrying a high exchange value
within local markets around the globe. In his famous *Histories*,
written between 450 and 420 BC, the Greek Herodotus records

Attic hoof vase, *c.* 470–460 BC.

the importance of beef as part of not only the social but also the economic life of civilizations, saying that in ancient Egypt each of the king's bodyguards was commonly paid with 'two pounds of beef' as part of their daily remuneration.

Today, cattle are present virtually in every country, on every continent in the world, and the consumption of beef forms the basis of many diets for hundreds of cultures. Many cattle breeds have been developed over the centuries specifically with beef consumption in mind. An example of this is the Chianina cattle in Italy, which – while having been known since the first century AD as a working breed – was specifically selected for intensive breeding in the early twentieth century; the particular fast-growing rates of this cattle make it the perfect specimen for the meat industry, giving great quantities of lean and high-quality beef. Another well-known and well-regarded breed is the Aberdeen Angus (or simply Angus), a

. was descended from cattle native to the Aberdeen-
    nd Angus regions of Scotland. This particular cattle was
    eloped by Scottish breeder Hugh Watson specifically for
    eef consumption in the mid-1800s, with the intention of
producing large quantities of very high-quality meat. Watson
selected the best specimens from Scottish cattle and obtained
what is known as the 'Angus' through selective and intensive
cross-breeding. In spite of its popularity not only in the UK,
but particularly also in the U.S., the quality of Aberdeen Angus
beef did not become protected until 1978, when a specification-
based, branded beef programme was initiated in order to produce what is known as Certified Angus Beef (CAB). Within the
food service industry, the term 'Angus Beef' is often misappro-
priated and confused with CAB. The latter, on the other hand,
is an appellative that can be given only to particular beef that
has been grown and reared in an establishment approved by
the American Angus Association and its British counterparts.

Across the globe, beef is consumed in a variety of ways,
producing a number of highly differing dishes, ranging from
elaborate concoctions of thin strips of meat, to hearty beef
stews and family-feeding barbecues. It is not only the flesh of
cattle that is consumed; beef is used as the basis of several
meat by-products such as beef gravy and beef tea. A myriad of
national and internationally known dishes containing beef can
be found throughout the world. The impact of immigration
and open-trade markets – especially in the post-industrialist
era of the twentieth century – have allowed beef and beef
dishes to travel across geographical boundaries. The burger,
one of the most famous and infamous incarnations of beef
in the modern world, is a known food that can be recognized
in virtually every country, the American version given by fast
food chains often surpassing in knowledge more traditional
and homemade variations of the beef patty. But the burger,

An Aberdeen Angus bull. This particular breed is often the star of cattle competitions, where the best specimens are showcased and later sold at astronomical prices.

however, is not the only manifestation of beef that has a claim to fame. Well-known dishes such as beef Wellington, beef bourguignon and beef stroganoff have conquered the eating habits of populations throughout the globe, largely transcending and exceeding their respective places of origin in Britain, France and Russia.

How Beef Got its Name

In the modern English language, the word 'beef' owes its origins to factors and circumstances that are all but English. Etymologically speaking, the word 'beef' is derived from Latin; the ancient Romans referred to the meat of cattle as *bubula*. This was in contrast to the term *bovus*, which was commonly used to refer to anything pertaining to oxen and cows. The influence of the Latin terminology is clearly still evident today, its impact unmissable in everyday words such as 'bovine', and more scientific terms such as '*Bovinae*', identifying a biological sub-family that includes various forms of hoofed animals, from domestic cattle to yaks, water buffalos and American bison.

And yet, in spite of the similarities between Latin *bubula* and our beef, the connection between the two is not as straightforward as one might think. The Romans did conquer Britain and left much evidence of their empire when they left the land in AD 410. However, a direct use of the Latin language was not one such legacy. Indeed, by the time Old English emerged as an early incarnation of the language we use today, Germanic influences had all but revolutionized grammar, terminologies and common references. By the seventh century, the Latin *bubula* had long been left behind and early English speakers referred to cattle and their meat by the Anglo-Saxon *cu*, a term that would develop into the Middle English *cou*, a not-so-early ancestor of our 'cow'. While this development is

Heracles/Theseus and the Cretan Bull, *c.* 490–480 BC, Attic vase.

unsurprising, it does not answer the question of how beef became known as such. For an answer, we need to skip to 1066, to the battle of Hastings and the Norman-French invasion. As William the Conqueror claimed the shores of Britain, he also laid claim to its language. After the conquest, the Norman aristocracy that took control of England had no interest in adopting the local Anglo-Saxon idiom, as it was perceived to be inappropriate for any form of nobility or genteel expression. As the French nobles shunned the use of the common *cou* to refer to the meat of cattle, they opted for their own *boef* – a derivative of the Latin term *bubula* and an ancestor of the modern French word *boeuf*. While various manifestations of the Anglo-Saxon *Cou* remained in use among peasants to refer to live cows, Norman-French speakers – the most common consumers of the animals' flesh who, however, did not often deal with the live beasts – established their own *boef* as a suitable term for the meat. The dichotomy became established in Britain and *cou* and *boef* co-existed in everyday expression. Through a convoluted etymological journey, then, the meat of cattle found its own seating within the English language, developing through the ages and becoming what has been known for centuries as 'beef'.

Beef and the Romans

The Romans did not have a particular predilection for beef. It was eaten rarely and, even then, it maintained a clear mark of luxury. Reserved for special occasions, beef was often connected to religious ceremonies. A cow was seen as a very apt sacrifice for the gods and its immolation was treated with the highest respect and consideration, especially during the festival known as *tauralia*. The animal was slaughtered ritually and while some of its prime parts were actually burned at the altar and 'reserved' for the gods, the organs – such as the heart, the liver and the lungs – would be given to the priests, so that they could partake in the ancient ritual of sharing food with the deity, an act that commemorated kinship.

Religious ritual, however, was not the only obstacle that the popularity of beef encountered among the Roman population. Indeed, behind the lack of preference for bovine meat

Mithras slaying a sacrificial ox, 2nd century AD. The killing of the astral bull, also known as *tauroctony*, was at the centre of the Hellenic and Roman cult of Mithras.

there was a much more mundane, logistical reasoning. Cows were difficult to keep because of their size. They required pastures and the Romans preferred to use land for agriculture and the growth of grains. By virtue of their size, cows also needed to be tended to in various ways that were not required by other animals. So the maintenance of cattle was laborious, time-consuming and not so cost-effective.

In addition, beef was difficult to preserve. Refrigeration techniques were not developed in Roman times and cows, because of their size, would provide large amounts of meat, which proved a challenge. Cold weather was required to keep the beef fresh, and the fact that the Mediterranean region was hot almost year-round meant that it did not prove fitting for the task of beef preservation. So, naturally, the Romans opted for other meats – pork, known as *sus* or *porcus*, was the most popular among the plebeian population, while the Roman patricians often opted for extravagant, luxurious and highly prized meats such as ostrich and peacock.

All the same, one should not think that the Romans did not eat beef at all. Generally speaking, cows were kept mainly for fieldwork and dairy consumption, but that does not mean that the meat was shunned. A penchant for veal was particularly prevalent. The famous *Apicius* or *De re Coquinaria* – one of the earliest surviving recipe books from Roman times – cites a number of recipes involving beef, such as *bubulam cum porris* (beef with leeks) and *bubula fricta* (fried beef steak).

Beef in Europe

Following the influence of the Roman conquest – and subsequent fall of the Roman Empire – beef gained an incremental favour among many European populations. Cattle were raised throughout the continent, both as livestock for meat and dairy products, and as draft animals. The popularity of cattle in Europe had a great impact on rural and urban practices in several countries. Germanic peoples were particularly fond of beef. Viking tribes – flourishing between AD 700 and 900 – were known to exploit all parts of the cow, from using its skin to make leather goods to consuming the flesh of the animal in the form of roasts and stews.

Within the British Isles, the Anglo-Saxons had a distinct predilection for beef, but their interest in the meat seems somewhat curious. Indeed, beef was often consumed for its therapeutic properties. In the *Bald's Leechbook*, a domestic manual dating from around AD 95, several 'recipes' are listed that include beef; these, however, must be interpreted more as curative remedies than delicious dishes to be consumed for their gastronomic value. The imagistic connection between cow and strength clearly made an impression on the way in which the Anglo-Saxons perceived beef, building a belief that meat deriving from cattle would bestow health upon those who ate it.

The Anglo-Saxons, however, were not the only ones to maintain a conviction that beef could cure disease. As Anglo-Saxon lands evolved into what would later become England, beef retained curative properties in the popular imagination. From the sixteenth century onwards, in particular, a large number of British domestic manuals list beef as a principal medical ingredient. The meat was prescribed to 'feed a fever' in the form of beef-based soups and teas. In the eighteenth century, patients suffering from various ailments were often advised to drink 'beef tonics'. Undoubtedly encouraged by the fear of tuberculosis in the late nineteenth century, popular belief in the invigorating power of beef-based concoctions continued until the early twentieth century, when beef tonics became widely advertised as an essential way to enrich and revitalize the blood.

Beef, however, was not simply enjoyed as a medical marvel. Numerous examples of beef recipes (to be consumed for their gastronomic value) can be found in famous historical cookbooks, such as the French *Le Viandier* – dating from around 1300 – and the English *Forme of Cury*, compiled by the Master-Cooks of Richard II in 1390. Although beef had an undeniable presence in late medieval life, it was by no means the favourite meat. Historical records show that beef took a secondary position to fish, chicken and pork, the latter being the most popular 'meat' as such. In the Iberian Peninsula, numerous Catalan cookbooks dating from around 1450 show that mutton was definitely the meat of choice for the local population, both common and aristocratic.

In the early decades of the Renaissance, and following the Black Death's devastating impact on farming and agriculture, meat derived from cattle was subjected to a distinct revival in favour. In fourteenth- and fifteenth-century Italy, veal was particularly appreciated as a 'summer meat', its lighter texture and flavour making it a more delectable option than beef's earthy and wintery appeal. Overall, beef was regarded as too coarse for the refined upper classes, which preferred to consume delicate and visually pleasing meats such as heron and swan. The extravagant tastes of the aristocracy grew exponentially after the discovery of America in 1492, when exotic ingredients such as vanilla, peanuts and novel breeds of fowl began to attract the attention of many noble gourmands.

The role of beef as a 'peasant meat' survived until the nineteenth century. British cookbooks prove that ever since the Middle Ages beef has been used as a filling for pies. In eighteenth-century England, the meat even evolved into a popular food for the masses within cities. Beef pies were known have been sold in the streets of London as a quick and affordable meal. Beef – cheaply purchased in large quantities – was often the vendors' favourite ingredient because their customers were numerous enough to consume the product of a slaughtered cow in a matter of days. Street-sold pies were extremely popular and, in a way, functioned as the beginning of beef's longstanding relationship with 'fast food'.

Beef in America

Being American is to eat a lot of beef steak, and boy, we've got a lot more beef steak than any other country, and that's why you ought to be glad you are an American.

Kurt Vonnegut

As difficult as it might be to imagine today, beef is a relatively recent addition to the American diet. Cattle were not indigenous to the American continent, and while herds of wild bison roamed the prairies and were consumed by Native American tribes for centuries, domesticated cattle did not actually reach the shores of the New World until the Spanish conquistadors introduced them in 1540. In 1623, two Devon heifers and a Devon bull were imported to the Plymouth Colony from Britain. Although mainly used for dairy produce and fieldwork, Devon cattle were highly valued in the American colonies. One has to wait until the early eighteenth century in order to witness cattle systematically raised in farms by the colonists – likely of Spanish, French and British origin – for consumption purposes. As the new American country grew, so did its infrastructure, allowing early American examples of the cattle industry to blossom, develop and fortify. By 1871, new refrigeration methods allowed the transportation

Frederic Remington, 'Roasting the Christmas Beef in a Cavalry Camp', drawing from *Harper's Weekly* (1892).

of meat to be an easy enough task and, as a result, the cattle industry was radically transformed. A number of slaughterhouses were quickly established across the Midwest and shipments of meat to all corners of the country regularly took place. As the demand for cattle meat quickly replaced the existing (and by no means erased) preference for chicken and pork, beef was given a prominent position on American tables, from San Antonio to New Orleans, from Detroit to New York. During and after the Second World War, the cattle industry reached its apogee and beef became a ready symbol for American affluence. Beef's aesthetic qualities allowed it to become a metaphorical representation of American sanguinity and American science was only too obliging in confirming the meat's nutritional qualities, including its high content of essential protein. It was estimated that by 1952, the average American consumed 28 kg (62 lb) of beef a year. Finding its most American of incarnations in the hamburger patty, beef became incorporated into the American diet to such an extent

...ne historian Josh Ozersky defines the beefburger as the ...erican 'meal par excellence'.

By the time the 1960s were in full swing, beef had taken on a role that pushed its boundaries beyond its gastronomic merits. In the midst of the Cold War, beef became a powerful symbol in propaganda. In 1960, a famous promotional movie entitled *Beef Rings the Bell* proclaimed that beef steaks and burgers were an 'American institution'. Running on the assumption that the audience adored beef – as was probably the case – *Beef Rings the Bell* encouraged consumers to support the American cattle industry by eating beef on a regular basis, an act that, aside from bringing economic prosperity to the country, was levelled as a signifier of expected patriotism. The propagandist intentions of the beef campaigns in the 1960s clearly had the desired effect on the population and, while the cattle industry continued to boom, by 1970 the average American was eating 50 kg (110 lb) of beef a year, almost twice the amount that had been consumed only twenty years before.

Today, the u.s. produces about 25 per cent of the world's beef supply with – somewhat surprisingly – less than 10 per cent of the world's cattle population. Across the land, Texas remains the top beef-producing state.

Argentine Beef

The cattle industry in Argentina has a long and established history. Indeed, beef is such an integral part of the culture of Argentina, both materially and metaphorically, that one might venture to say that consuming the meat is part of being Argentinian. As was the case with North America, cattle were not indigenous to South America. Cattle were introduced to what is now Argentina in the early sixteenth century by –

unsurprisingly – Spanish conquistadors, who obviously had a penchant for taking their cows and oxen with them wherever they went. The Argentine pampas proved an excellent geographical set-up for the herds of cattle that were left to roam and, as a result of underdeveloped infrastructures, the cow population grew quickly. With time, however, local landowners capitalized on the production of beef and, over a relatively short period, the cattle industry flourished. By the eighteenth century, Argentina had established itself as the biggest producer and consumer of beef in Latin America. Once the nineteenth century arrived, technology once again proved the most important factor in the part beef played in the country's economy. Railway construction aided the establishment of commercial infrastructures and, thanks to the newly arrived refrigeration cars, beef could be transported over large geographical areas, causing the Argentinian beef industry to thrive on an international scale. By 1886, Argentinian beef was in high demand and the geographical position of the country – located in the Southern hemisphere – allowed

Gauchos herding cattle in the Patagonia region of Argentina.

the meat to be available at times when European and American beef was 'out of season'.

With such an imposing presence in the economic fabric of the country, beef inevitably also played an essential part in the historical development of local customs, traditions and, at times, even folklore. Culturally speaking, eating habits and festivities in Argentina developed in connection with beef. The ever-local *asado* – the term used for a range of barbecuing techniques in Argentina, also giving its name to a popular social event – emerged concomitantly with the development of the beef industry. While the meats cooked as part of an *asado* festivity also included a wide range of pork and chicken cuts, beef towered uncontested as the favourite, therefore creating a cultural association between its consumption and a much-beloved, perhaps romanticized, vision of community and family life. And the romanticization of beef in Argentina does not stop at eating. The prominent figure of the gaucho – a pampas-dwelling, brooding, poncho-wearing Argentinean who is a loose equivalent of the American cowboy – is surrounded by an ever-growing number of stories about courage and bravado, associating all elements of the beef industry with a sense of Argentinian pride, patriotism and almost melancholy attachment to the past.

Unsurprisingly, as undeniable economic advantages and passionate tales of pampas heroism interweave in the history of the country's cattle industry, beef still maintains its hold on Argentina's way of life today. In 2006, it was estimated that Argentinians were the world's second-largest consumers of beef per capita, with the average Argentinian eating 55 kg (121 lb) of beef per year. The Argentinian cattle industry maintains a reputation for producing very high-quality beef. As a result, Argentina is the third-largest exporter of beef in the world, after Brazil and Australia. The dream of the gaucho

roaming the pampas, guarding the cattle and gazing at t
stars lives on, it would seem. I wonder if the cows are just as
starstruck. Probably not.

Japanese Beef

I know what you are thinking. You know your cows. Japanese beef is highly prized, a special category of meat that is
coveted and expensive and served only in the best and most
fashionable restaurants around the world. You are imagining
television chefs singing the praises of Kobe beef and pro-
claiming its superior qualities. And you are probably assuming,
just as I did, that the Japanese might have been perfecting 'the
art of beef' for centuries, perhaps even millennia. As it turns
out, the history of beef in Japan is not longstanding; it is,
without a doubt, a modern development.

Prior to the year 1868, eating the flesh of four-legged
animals was prohibited in Japan. Since the country showcases
strong Buddhist influences, the prohibition does not come as
a surprise. The ban over eating large farm animals became
particularly strict during what is known as the Edo period
(1603–1867) in order to support the development of agriculture. Over time, the religious influence on food prohibitions
became entangled with cultural parameters and the consumption of beef was perceived as a national taboo. Nonetheless,
things changed radically in 1867 with the ascent to the throne
of Emperor Meiji. The new emperor had a desire to build
strong relations – particularly of an economic nature – with
the West and regarded the consumption of beef as an essential part of his political strategy. Wanting to reduce the traditional social and cultural barriers that separated Japan from
countries such as the u.s., Emperor Meiji lifted the ban on beef

Kobe beef, photographed before cooking at a restaurant in Japan.

and encouraged its consumption among the population. While pork remained the meat of choice across the country, beef-eating slowly became more prevalent in the early twentieth century. Specifically, the inhabitants of the Kinki Region – which included Kyoto, Kobe and Osaka – were known to be, and still are today, the heaviest beef eaters in the country. Japanese folklore has it that the consumption of beef was carried out in the Kobe region as a secret ritual even during the times of the beef ban, with famous shoguns showing a predilection for the prized meat. While little historical evidence exists in support of this claim, the preference for Kobe beef throughout Japan after the Meiji culinary revolution is difficult to argue.

Kobe beef traditionally comes from *wagyu* cattle. The appellative of 'Kobe' refers to the geographical region where this type of herd was first reared. '*Wa*' is an ancient Japanese term for Japan, and one of the meanings of '*gyu*' is beef, with a specific 'on the hoof' connotation. Currently, there are five principal breeds of *wagyu* cattle in Japan: Japanese

Blacks, Japanese Browns, Japanese Polls, Japanese Lc
horns and Kumamoto Reds. These breeds are not stric.
native to the country and are the result of a substantia.
infusion of European blood during the Meiji era. After 1910,
however, the importing of European breeds ceased and it
was not until the Second World War that the Japanese government began to encourage the registration of cattle exhibiting
superior traits from both foreign and native types. In 1948,
the National Wagyu Cattle Registration Association was established and the production of beef became the focus of careful
screening programmes aimed at producing the best-quality
meat in Japan.

Genetically speaking, *wagyu* cattle have a disposition to
hold a higher percentage of omega 3 fatty acids. This fact is
responsible for the marbled appearance of the meat, which
not only functions as the trademark of Kobe beef but also
bestows upon the meat its distinctive taste. The natural soft-
ness of Kobe beef is encouraged in the industry by adding a
small amount of sake to the cattle's feed and massaging their
muscles to support the iconic marbling. The latter fact has given
birth to the conception that *wagyu* cattle are the most pampered
cows in the industry, enjoying the many benefits of true Japanese hospitality.

In spite of Japan's cultural attachment to Kobe beef, however, most *wagyu* cattle are not actually raised in Japan. While
for decades the Japanese government prohibited the export
of any live *wagyu* cattle in an attempt to protect and safeguard
the quality of Kobe beef, four *wagyu* animals were imported
to the United States in 1976. By 1993, California had become
the greatest producers of Kobe beef in the world. By 2001,
Australia also claimed its place as a high-profile producer of
Kobe beef. Today, both the u.s. and Australia have an accord
with the Japanese Wagyu Association so that they can raise

_/ cattle and produce Kobe beef for world export and ..sumption under strict laws. One of these laws demands ..at _wagyu_ cattle be raised within specific parameters and that the traditional methods for obtaining Kobe marbling be respected – with muscle massages as a strict priority. The pampering of _wagyu_ cattle, whether taking place in Japan or any other corner of the world, clearly still has its desired effect and Kobe beef maintains its status as a highly coveted delicacy.

Beef Down Under

In Australia, the beef cattle industry is one of the most profitable areas of the country's economy, generating more than $3 billion a year. The beef industry has been prevalent in Australia since its colonial origins and beef has been intertwined with the country's growth and development for centuries. Cattle were first brought to Australia on the First Fleet, which came from Britain in 1788. The Fleet's aim was to bring people to the newly 'discovered' Australian continent and establish the first settlements for British colonists. Cattle travelled with them and laid their claim to the Australian economy very early on. In the initial years of the colonies, however, the intended use of cattle was for fieldwork and transport. Australian rural folklore has it that in the early 1790s, a few specimens of cattle strayed and were found several years later, the numbers of their wild herd having grown to 60. There is no evidence to either discard or assure this claim; what is known, however, is that by 1820 there were already 54,000 cattle in Australia, their number having spectacularly risen to six times this figure by 1840. The demand for beef, and the idea of using cattle for consumption on a large industrial scale, did not appear until the 1850s, when the Gold Rushes hit Australia and groups of hungry miners invaded its lands. As the demand for b grew quickly, Australian drovers moved their cattle her away from urban areas – Sydney in particular – and settl them as far as Western Australia. The cattle were known have travelled for weeks, often having to swim long distanc to reach their destinations.

By the time the twentieth century hit, Australia ha become a great beef producer, with its cattle industry boom ing as the country's greatest economic force. Today, the state of Queensland is the greatest producer of beef, with the meat coming from popular Hereford, Shorthorn and Murray Grey cattle. Australia, as a result, is one of the largest and most successful exporters of beef in the world. It goes without saying that the Australians enjoy beef immensely as well, making a cultural virtue of their beloved summer barbecues – a true Australian institution.

On the other side of the Tasman Sea, New Zealand also prides itself on a developing history of beef. Cattle were imported to New Zealand from the UK in 1814, when Reverend

Beef cattle roaming around the Brisbane Valley, Australia, 1914.

Samuel Marsden set up a mission station on the northern shores of the newly formed colony. As time passed, more Europeans settled in New Zealand and, in the early 1840s, more cattle were imported from Australia. Most of these were what used to be referred to as Durham, a breed that later developed into what are now commonly known as Shorthorn cattle. Traditionally, however, beef cattle have often taken a secondary position in the New Zealand farming industry, falling behind dairy cattle – which allowed the country to become one of the principal exporters of dairy products in the world – and, of course, sheep. As early as 1851, the ratio of sheep to beef cattle in New Zealand was six to one. The higher ratio remained steady for more than a century, and it reached its peak in the early 1960s, with sheep outnumbering cattle in the country by fourteen to one. However, by the mid-1980s, and after the government restructured the subsidisation schemes for farming, the numbers of beef cattle inhabiting the rolling hills of New Zealand grew dramatically. Since the 1990s, the export market has been the focus of the New Zealand beef industry. Indeed, it is estimated that New Zealand exports more than 80 per cent of its beef, a very impressive percentage. Overall, New Zealand produces only 1 per cent of the world's beef, but nevertheless supplies approximately 8 per cent of the global beef trade.

New Zealand cattle are mostly allowed to roam freely in green pastures that are mainly concentrated on the North Island of the country. Beef cattle are primarily grass-fed and not fattened on grain – the latter a health concern that has attracted the attention of animal welfare associations around the world and which, clearly, New Zealand as a beef-producing country is very keen to avoid. The general population of New Zealand has developed a distinct taste for beef over time; nonetheless, lamb still remains the meat of choice among Kiwis, who are very happy to supply beef of the highest standard and send it as an ambassador to promote the country's excellence in farming around the world.

2

How to Cook Beef

Beef and cow's meat ought to be boiled, and breast of veal also,
but the back . . . requires roasting.
Maestro Martino da Como, *Libro de Arte Coquinaria* (1467)

Beef can be cooked in a variety of ways. The meat's versatility
lies in its ability to reach different stages of cooking through
different preparation methods, which inevitably have an impact on the taste and therefore the dishes that can be produced. From roasting to grilling, from boiling to smoking,
beef allows itself to be manipulated by the culinary arts in
order to adapt to a multiplicity of circumstances. Different
cuts of beef are known to be suited to different cooking
methods and these pairings often owe more to the situations
in which a particular dish evolved, rather than simply being
related to matters of gustation and anatomic composition.

There are two main categories under which the methods
of preparing and cooking beef can be catalogued: 'dry heat'
and 'moist heat'. 'Dry heat' relates to any cooking technique by
which the heat is usually transferred to the meat without using
any form of moisture. Dry-heat cooking methods tend to
employ high temperatures, which hover around 200°C (392°F)
and can sometimes be even hotter. Under this category one

can find methods such as roasting, grilling, broiling, fry
and stir-frying. On the other hand, the category of 'moist h
usually encompasses a variety of preparation methods that
on some type of liquid in order to cook the beef. The li
can vary from steam and water to wine and stock. Typical tecn-
niques which fall under this culinary umbrella include braising,
stewing and *sous vide*.

The typical brown appearance of cooked beef – achieved
through what is known as the 'Maillard reaction' – can generally only be gained through cooking the meat using a dry-heat
method. The browning, however, is not meant to be a simple
aesthetic quality of dry-heat-prepared beef. The contention
is that there is a direct correlation between browned beef and
exceptional taste, sporting rich flavours and deep aromas
that cannot generally be achieved through moist-heat cooking methods.

The majority of cooking methods for preparing beef are
ancient in nature and have evolved over the centuries in order
to suit not only the changing palates and demands of the
world populations, but also the sociocultural and anthropological issues that have been connected to the consumption
of beef over the ages.

Rare, Medium, Well Done

From the seventeenth century onwards, cookbook writers
began to warn their readers against the dangers of under-
cooked meat. When it came to beef, the preference was still
for what we would today define as 'well done' meat. Although
many examples of steak recipes can be found, the propensity
was still to cook and consume well-cooked beef in the form of
stews or roasts. Overall, instructions on how to achieve the

ideal appearance and flavour were still reliant on the cook's ability to monitor and check the meat. It was not until the nineteenth century that food scientists actually began to examine the various levels at which beef can be cooked. It was also during this time that specific instructions on temperatures and cooking times began to appear, in order to achieve the coveted texture, consistency and taste for the beef dish to be served. However, it was the early twentieth century that witnessed a true commitment to the cooking of beef in what was seen as an appropriate and time-efficient manner. The first meat thermometers made a commercial appearance in the 1930s and, as they took the culinary scene by storm, they also took the art of guessing out of cooking beef.

The word 'rare' has replaced the earlier term 'underdone' when discussing the cooking of beef. Without too much speculation, one could assume that this shift happened as the word 'underdone' carries a number of negative connotations with it, suggesting that the meat was not ready to be consumed. 'Rare', on the other hand, specifically refers to beef that has been lightly cooked, in order to suit the taste of diners and, at times, the specific requirements of creating beef dishes. In the English language, the term was thought for a long time to be an Americanism. In 1861, G. F. Berkeley, an English sportsman, famously used the term in a humorous way to refer to its American origins. When questioned about a particular sporting technique, he replied: 'The wood-cock and snipe? Should be underdone, or what the Americans call "rare".' In reality, this particular description of beef was present in the English language long before Americans declared their independence. When used to describe the doneness of beef, the word 'rare' itself derives – according to the *Oxford English Dictionary* – from the old term 'rear; meaning precisely underdone or "imperfectly cooked"'. The word 'rear' was originally used in relation to eggs and it is only in its transition to 'rare' that it came to be associated with meat. The earliest account of the term being used in reference to beef appears in the *Countrey Contentments*, a cookbook complied in 1615; the author, Gervase Markham, warns the book's readers to check their beef constantly while it's cooking, 'for as too much rareness is not wholesome, so too much driness is not nourishing'.

The common association between rare beef and America was probably due to a matter of preference, rather than actual origin. This connection between the meat and the American nation was often painted – both by the British and a select group of 'refined Americans' – with a layer of distaste, almost as a testament to the social brutality of the nation. In 1902, Sarah Tyson Rorer – author of *Mrs Rorer's Cook Book* – dedicated a long section to how to prepare beef and noted (not without a certain amount of revulsion) that

> The American fashion of serving meat 'rare' is certainly objectionable . . . red meats may be served a little under-done. This does not mean that the blood must run from them as they are carved, but that they must be pink, juicy and tender.

While the propensity to use the word 'medium' to define a particular level of cooking for beef is not a twentieth-century characteristic – expressions such as 'medium-roast-ed' or 'medium-boiled' are already present in fifteenth- and sixteenth-century cookbooks – simple definitions such as 'medium rare', 'medium done' or simply 'medium' in relation to preference began to dominate cookbooks in the post-1900 era. In 1932, Bell Lowe's *Experimental Cookery* gave a lot of attention to the stages of preparation that beef can achieve, specifically referring to such stages as 'Rare, Medium and Well

Done'. Lowe clearly states that this particular meat is one of the few – if not the only one – that can be 'safely cooked as rare'. She also surveys the process by which heat alters the colour, the texture and the taste of beef, simply suggesting that the longer a piece of beef is cooked, 'the more the interior colour changes from pink or red to gray, and the greater the culinary losses'. In her *Joy of Cooking* (1936), Irma Rombauer signals the appearance in the kitchen of meat thermometers and offers a detailed description of how to use them to roast beef at various stages: 'rare, 140 degrees; medium, 160 degrees; well done, 170 degrees'.

Roasting

In historical terms, roasting itself is one of the earliest cooking techniques mastered by the human race. The first roasting feasts were organized in prehistory in front of an open fire and the site was often the centre of social life for our ancestors.

When it comes to beef, the relationship between this particular food and roasting is undoubtedly one that can pride itself in an impressive longevity. Roasting still remains one of the most common preparation methods for the meat, whether it is carried out on a rack over a live fire or a conventional home oven. Over the centuries, spits have not proven popular in the process of roasting beef. This is probably due to a logistical issue, as the sheer size of a whole cow does not make it suitable for the spit: it would require a very large spit indeed. While the practice of spit-roasting beef is not completely unknown in several instances throughout history – with Argentina being a particular exponent in this group – spits have found their greatest popularity in the cooking of smaller animals, such as pigs, goats, sheep and, of course, chickens. Racks, on the other hand, have proved an effective tool in the process of roasting beef, as they allow for larger pieces of the meat to be cooked at the same time.

With the advent in history of more sophisticated heating techniques, oven-roasting became a common way of preparing beef that is still very popular today. The oven allows for slower cooking of the beef, which maintains its natural moisture, bestowing upon the meat its most distinctive taste. Whether cooked in an oven or on an open fire, however, beef is usually placed on a rack. During roasting, it is usually basted

'Roasting', from *Tacuinum Sanitatis*. This 14th-century manuscript illustration depicts a common beef-roasting scene.

on the surface with butter, oil or lard, in order to reduce the loss of moisture. As a general rule, the meat is removed from the heat before it is fully cooked; it should be covered and left to rest for a short period of time. While the beef rests, the inside cooks even further, thanks to the residual heat. This phenomenon – often referred to as 'carry over cooking' – is said to retain the juices of the meat and enhance its flavour. In her *Mrs Beeton's Book of Household Management* (1861), Isabella Beeton praises the simplicity of roasting as the method to prepare beef par excellence. She shows a certain poetic attachment for what she sees in antiquity as 'the age of roasting', when the preparation of beef started to be aided by common utensils that allowed the meat to be prepared in a more sophisticated way.

Beef is perfectly suited to roasting since it is a good method for cooking large cuts of meat. Cuts of beef are commonly tied up with string prior to roasting. Tying is known to hold the meat together during roasting and allows the beef to maintain a circular profile, which encourages even cooking and makes the beef easier to carve once it is ready to be served. Today, the knot of choice for tying a cut of beef is the reef knot, usually formed by tying a right-handed overhand knot followed by a left-handed overhand knot. More traditionally, beef roasts would have been tied with the packer's knot, an ancient binding knot that is secured by tightening the string into a figure of eight around the standing part in such a way that both ends emerge from the same point. The ends are then pulled tight over the standing part and secured with one last overhand knot. While the packer's knot historically has not only been used in the culinary arts, its particular popularity as the knot of choice for tying beef roasts has granted the technique its common name of 'butcher's knot'.

The term 'roast beef' carries important cultural connotations that transcend its basic definition of being meat that has simply been roasted or baked in the oven. Historically, beef has been the 'national meat' of England. Roast beef has many patriotic connotations associated with it, which have been surviving in the country for centuries. And there is certainly no doubt in the fact that, as a nation, the British love beef. The meat has occupied a privileged position in the British diet for centuries. In 1698, the travelling Frenchman Henri Misson, who was visiting London at the time and observing the culinary habits of the British with a keen eye, poignantly stated:

> It is common practice, even among People of Good Substance, to have a huge Piece of Roast-Beef on Sundays, on which they stuff until they can swallow no more, and eat the rest cold, without any other victuals, the other six Days of the Week.

Overall, the tendency of the British population to consume large quantities of beef has generated scorn among other populations. A notable example concerns precisely the French, who have been known to refer to the British derogatively as *rosbif*, openly mocking the overactive preference for simple and straightforward roasted beef in the British Isles.

In 1817, William Kitchiner – author of the well-respected *Apicius Redivivus; Or, The Cook's Oracle* – recommended his readers to eat as much as 3 kg (6½ lb) of meat every week, in order to ensure good health. Beef was clearly selected as the most beneficial meat of choice. In his book, Kitchiner describes in detail how to prepare a 'noble sirloin of about fifteen pounds', taking special care in recommending that it should be placed by the cook on an open fire at least four hours before going to church on Sundays. Kitchiner's instructions state that the meat had to cook slowly on racks, hooks or on small spits, and the large quantities of beef prepared would feed the household not only as a hot roast on the Sunday itself, but also in the guise of stews, pie fillings and cold cuts for the rest of the week.

While Kitchiner's method notably shows a high level of respect for cuts of beef, which must be handled with special reverence, only the wealthiest members of the community could afford the luxury of a wide-open fire and large quantities of beef. The less well-off members of the population had to make do with preparing smaller portions of beef and it is a recorded fact that they would drop off their roasts to the local bakers on their way to church, so that the beef could be cooked in the cooling ovens. This particular practice is what began the association in Britain between Sunday and beef roasts, a strong connection that is still maintained and respected in the country today.

The meat has been part of the British diet for so long that its image has permeated many of the most distinctive features of the country. At the Tower of London, the Yeoman Warders – the royal bodyguards – have been known as 'beefeaters' since the fifteenth century. There are many explanations for this; in folklore, the guards are said to have been paid in beef, therefore giving them the affectionate and well-known appellative. A later historical source attributes the creation of the name to Count Cosimo, the Grand Duke of Tuscany, who visited the Tower in 1669, and is said to have commented: 'A very large ration of beef is given to them daily at court . . . that they might be called Beef-eaters.'

The presence and impact of roast beef, however, cannot be measured in Britain alone. The traditional beef Sunday lunch is a common meal in several countries around the

The quintessential Sunday lunch: roast beef served with vegetables, gravy and Yorkshire puddings.

world, particularly those which historically have had a strong connection with the former British Empire, such as the U.S., Canada, Ireland, New Zealand and Australia. In the countries that used to be British colonies, however, roast beef has refused to simply stay in its traditional incarnation. While examples of the Sunday dinner still remain popular, roast beef has also been served in a variety of different ways. In the U.S., for instance, roast beef is a very popular filling for sandwiches. A well-known example is the 'beef on weck' sandwich, which is found primarily in the western New York area. Although its precise origins are not clear, the 'beef on weck' sandwich is said to have come from Buffalo in the early 1800s. This particular roast beef sandwich is German in origin and is said to have been introduced to the Buffalo culinary scene by a German immigrant who owned a bar. *Weck* is the Southern German word for roll. The sandwich is made with roast beef on a *kummelweck* roll. The beef is usually served rare and the bun is often dipped in the meat's *jus*.

Grilling

Grilling is another popular way of cooking beef. It employs dry heat, which is usually applied to the meat either from above or from below. As grilling is a form of 'direct heat' cooking, the temperatures involved can reach in excess of 260°C (500°F). The meat tends to be cut into pieces or slices before it is exposed to the heat, and it is usually cooked on a grill, a griddle or a griddle pan. A grill tends to have an open grid with the heat source coming from both directions. With this system, the heat is transferred onto the beef primarily through what is known as thermal radiation. A griddle, on the other hand, is a flat plate with the heat source coming from below. Finally, a griddle pan – which is very similar in concept to a frying pan – has raised ridges that allow it to mimic the cooking effects of an open grill. These last two grilling methods differ in concept from the open grill in that they rely on direct heat induction being transferred onto the beef.

In the UK, and several other Commonwealth countries such as Australia and New Zealand, 'grilling' is the term used to refer to cooking beef directly under a source of dry heat. Especially in Britain, 'the grill' is a specific part of the oven, and is often granted its own, self-standing layer. Grilling in an electric oven, however, can be a dissatisfying experience. Apart from the inconvenience of having to keep the oven door open, grilling beef in an electric oven causes a lot of smoke and splattering of fat and oil. The contention is that the meat also does not present its distinctive grilled flavour, remaining blander if undoubtedly easier to cook.

In Japan, a popular way of consuming beef is in the form of *yakiniku*, a way of cooking and serving which broadly refers to all grilled meat dishes. Widespread throughout Japan, *yakiniku* restaurants are mostly likely derived from an original group of Korean restaurants which opened in Osaka and Tokyo in 1945 – although several chefs in Japan refute this contention, claiming that the grilling method and the *yakiniku* dishes that derive from it are strictly Japanese in origin. The base for a *yakiniku* meal usually consists of beef and offal, with chuck slices, ribs and tripe being principal ingredients. The meat is cut into small pieces and cooked on griddles and gridirons over a low flame of wood charcoal. Recently, pork has also begun to make an appearance as an additional ingredient at *yakiniku* restaurants; in spite of this, however, beef remains the favourite meat of choice for this particular grilling method. At *yakiniku* restaurants, the meat is chosen by the patrons and is taken directly to their table still in its raw form. The diners themselves cook the pieces of beef and offal on a grill. The cooked meat is then dipped in a variety of soy-based sauces, known collectively as *tare*, before being eaten. The popularity of *yakiniku* in Japan has become so widespread since its inception in the 1940s that in 1993 the All Japan Yakiniku Association (*Zenkoku Yakiniku Kyoukai*) proclaimed 29 August to be the official 'Yakiniku Day'.

Yakiniku bears a close resemblance to the Korean *bulgogi* (or *bul go gi*), a dish consisting of beef, usually sirloin, marinated in a mixture of soy sauce, sesame oil, sugar, garlic, peppers and mushrooms. The beef is traditionally grilled with garlic, onions and chopped green peppers; noodles are also often added as an accompaniment. *Bulgogi* is said to have originated during the Goguryeo era (37 BC–AD 668), when grilled beef became a popular food. The long history of the dish means that it has seen many changes and adaptations over time. Its contemporary incarnation is derived from a mixture of its original Goguryeo manifestation of grilled beef – which was referred to as *maekjeok* – and *neobiani*, a dish

Yakiniku beef grill.

of 'thinly spread' beef which was popular among the aristocracy in the Joseon Dynasty (1392–1897). In the modern age, *bulgogi* has often been served with a salad or – even more commonly in recent years – as the base for a Korean version of the hamburger, where the burger patty is prepared in the traditional *bulgogi* marinade before being grilled.

Grilling finds its most common and well-known incarnation in the barbecue. In this particular method, ancient in

origin, the heat source comes exclusively from below the meat. There are several examples of barbecuing instruments and techniques that commonly cook beef around the world, including the Japanese *hibachi* – a cylindrical open-top container designed to hold burning charcoal and originating in the Heian period (AD 794–1185) – and the Middle Eastern kebab, a special dish of grilled meat displayed on a large skewer. In etymological terms, the English term barbecue has evolved from *barbacoa*, a form of cooking meat that

A modern interpretation of the Korean *bulgogi*.

originated in the Caribbean; the word literally means 'sacred fire pit'.

While in itself a barbecue can be composed of several meats, with pork often being the meat of choice, there are instances in which a barbecue 'means' beef. An example of this is the well-known Texas barbecue, where beef surpasses any other type of meat in preference and is cooked on open grills, allowing for several larger pieces of meat to be prepared at the same time. The propensity of Texans to prefer beef should not come as a surprise, since the state prides itself on having the highest numbers of cattle in the whole country. An all-beef barbecue in the u.s. is also often referred to as a 'cowboy barbecue'; the choice of meat is also reflected in the tendency to employ more direct heat forms and to use barbecues with larger grilling areas.

Indeed, a beef barbecue is not, paradoxically, just a matter of beef. It is often a social event, the word 'barbecue' signalling a gathering of family and friends where meat will be present. On occasion, however, the most sought-after quality of 'the barbecue' is not necessarily the grilled meat, but the event itself. The barbecue as social function takes many shapes and forms around the world, although, admittedly, on all these occasions meat is more likely to be served than not. A significant exponent within this category is the South African *braai*. The term is an Afrikaans word meaning literally 'to grill'. The word has been widely adopted by English speakers in South Africa and is usually interchangeable with the term 'barbecue'. Although several meats can be cooked as part of the *braai* grill, beef takes a special place on the list of ingredients. The fact that beef's flavour is enhanced when it is barbecued, and the widespread presence of cattle throughout South Africa, have transformed beef into the *braai* meat par

Carl Rudolf Huber, *Cattle Herd Under Pollarded Willows*, late 19th century, oil on canvas.

excellence. Beef is prepared on a variety of *braai* grills, all of which maintain the barbecuing prerogative of having the heat source coming from below. The 'skottel *braai*', a particular concave solid metal surface on legs, is particularly favoured for barbecuing beef, as the sauces and meat juices which escape during cooking are collected in the dip and can be re-used repeatedly for basting. The kettle grill is also particularly favoured for the beef *braai*, as the domed shape allows larger cuts of meat to cook thoroughly.

However, and in spite of its obvious feeding function, the *braai* is above all a social occasion and custom. The event is dictated by specific social norms; women, for instance, are rarely known to cook the *braai*, maintaining (as in many areas of the Western world) the almost prehistoric cultural associ-ation between men and grilled meat. Traditionally, while the men gather around the *braai* with trays of beef, the women pre-pare the accompaniments and the trimmings, such as salads, vegetables and desserts. The customary importance of the *braai* as an icon of cultural heritage is even commemorated in South Africa with '*Braai* Day', which is widely celebrated on 24 Sept-ember. The beauty of the *braai* is that it enables the host to be at the centre of attention around the grill, allowing for social mingling and entertainment. And, in so doing, the *braai* also highlights beef's longstanding ability to act as an unbreakable bonding agent, recalling the open fires and close tribal connec-tions of our Neolithic ancestors.

Broiling

Broiling is a method of cooking beef that is usually classed as a sub-category of grilling. In reality, there are some fundamen-tal differences between the two processes, which allow them to be seen as two separate ways of preparing the meat. Many modern recipes for beef suggest 'broiling' instead of grilling, but fail to identify the basic distinctions and similarities that can make a cooking session either a success or a failure. Like grilling, broiling relies on the use of radiant dry heat. And like grilling, broiling necessitates direct heat and high temperatures to cook the beef; both methods, therefore, require a watchful eye on the cook's part in order to avoid burning or excessive drying. Both methods also allow the beef to acquire a similar level of caramelization and charring which give the meat one of its most distinctive flavours. Unlike grilling, however, broiling is usually done indoors – commonly in the oven – and is very convenient if an open grill in the garden proves a difficult tool to find or operate. A broiler pan is to be used when broiling beef in the oven. Traditionally, a broiler pan comes in two pieces, a deeper, solid lower pan – known as a drip pan – and a slotted upper pan. As a cooking method relying on dry heat, broiling is not known to particularly soften the fibres of beef, and it is not usually recommended for 'tougher' cuts of meat.

The term 'broiling' is most likely derived from the Old French '*bruller*' (to roast or to burn). The Middle English word 'broillen' appears commonly in fourteenth-century culinary records, likely used as synonym for 'cook'. In North America, there is a tendency to refer to all forms of grilling as 'broiling', which often causes confusion. Historically, gridirons were employed to broil beef and other meats in the oven. Many of the practices that are common, albeit ill-advised, when broiling beef today – such as scoring the beef, or even basting – are strongly opposed in a number of historical cookbooks. In *The Art of Cookery Made Plain and Easy* (1784), Hannah Glasse warned prospective cooks 'never to baste anything on the gridiron, for it only makes it smoked and burnt'. The quality and preservation of the gridirons are also granted particular attention on several occasions, as the blackened quality of a misused iron is said to affect the taste and texture of the broiled beef. In *The Servant's Guide and Family Manual* (1831), cooks were also warned to keep their gridirons polished and 'bright' before and after broiling, since 'there is no good cause for the bars ever becoming black'. Once it reached the irons and was put in the oven, the beef had to be greased with lard to stop sticking, and 'to prevent the meat from being marked by the gridirons' (*The Cook's Own Book*, 1832).

Smoke was viewed as an extremely detrimental side-effect of broiling beef, a perspective that is still maintained today. Fires were to be kept clear and vigorous at all times. In *Buckmaster's Cookery* (1984), we are offered a good tip to avoid our beef from producing smoke and engulfing the kitchen:

> When the fat smokes and blazes too much remove the gridiron for an instant, and just sprinkle the fire with a little salt. Arrange your gridiron, if possible, so that it may be from two to five inches above the fire and slightly inclined towards the cook.

In terms of handling the meat, historical cookbooks suggest using 'steak tongs' (or even simply fingers) rather than a fork in order to avoid breaking the surface of the beef and causing the juices to run out. In *The Complete Servant* (1826), Samuel and Sarah Adams dedicate a sizeable part of their writing to the preparation of beef and suggest 'broiling it quick and turn[ing] it often, with steak-tongs, to keep in the gravy and make it a nice brown'.

The name 'London Broil' is used to describe a famous dish consisting of a marinated and quick-broiled flank steak. The meat is then cut across the grain and served in thin strips. In spite of its name, the dish is completely American in origin and is unknown in Britain. Indeed, the very few instances in which 'London Broil' appears in British cookbooks make clear that the dish is North American and continue to refer to it as such. The origins of the dish are still shrouded in mystery and all that is known is that it was introduced in American culinary books sometime during the years of the Great Depression. Renowned food historian John Mariani has observed that the first instance of 'London Broil' appearing in print dates to 1931, as a feature in Charles G. Shaw's 'Nightlife: *Vanity Fair*'s Intimate Guide to New York'. Plenty of American butchers have been known over the years to refer to a particular cut of beef as 'London Broil'; this is, however, a misinterpretation of the term. London Broil is not, in fact, a cut of meat at all. It is a recipe, a way of preparing and serving beef. As Merle Ellis of the *Los Angeles Times* declared in 1979: 'Cattle don't have London Broils. Recipe books have London Broils.' For decades, flank steak was considered synonymous with 'London Broil', as this particular

Alfred Grey Hochlandrinder, *Highland Cattle*, 1887, oil on canvas.

cut was the most commonly used in preparing the dish. In recent years, however, top round roasts have been erroneously labelled as 'London Broil', together with other various cuts of beef – such as sirloin, chuck or shoulder clod – which have been known to be marketed as the perfect base for this particular recipe. In 1973, the National Livestock and Meat Board in the u.s. issued an official recommendation for the appellative of 'London Broil' to be removed when butchers were merchandising beef, as its various incarnations were a source of confusion for the consumers. Nonetheless, 'London Broil' still makes a regular appearance in butchers' shops in America as a particular product that one can purchase. The cuts' disparities across the States are clearly not a deterrent in the marketing campaigns for the beef.

The preparation of the steak to be used in 'London Broil' is labour intensive. As the muscle fibres run through the entire length of this cut – in instances where the intended flank steak is actually used – the beef can become tough if it is not appropriately tenderized prior to cooking. Massaging and pounding are an essential part of preparing the steak, not only making it easier to cook, but also rendering it more tender when being cut and consumed. Marinating the flank steak – in a traditional mixture of vinegar, sugar, garlic and oil – is also an essential part of the preparation of 'London Broil'. In spite of the fact that many suggestions relating to their usefulness appear in American cookbooks – especially those written in the 1950s, such as the *Good Housekeeping Cook Book* (1955) – other preparation methods such as stabbing and scoring are not recommended in the preparation on 'London Broil', since the cuts inflicted on the beef before it is cooked cause the meat to become very tough, as essential juices and moisture are allowed to escape from the beef flank and run into the broiling pan.

While 'London Broil' is an American invention, a curious version of the dish can be found throughout Canada. This variety sees a ground beef patty being wrapped in flank steak. While the 'beef on beef' concoction remains the most popular throughout the country, some Canadian butchers have been known to use a pork sausage patty as the filler, while maintaining the beef flank steak as the wrapping sheet. In Ontario, another variety of the dish – known commonly as 'London Broil loaf' – has the flank beef steak wrapped around a spiced portion of ground veal.

Stewing

A stew is usually a combination of meat and vegetables which is allowed to cook in liquid in a casserole dish over a period of time and is served with the gravy that results from the cooking process. Beef is a favoured meat for this dish, since the strong nature of the meat means it tends not to lose its flavour while cooking for longer times. Tougher cuts are particularly suited to this method of preparation, since the meat is allowed to cook slowly and tenderize so that it literally 'falls off' the bone. Stewing is a form of low-cost cooking, as the wet heat permits the use of cheaper cuts, which are softened with time without losing any moisture. A method of preparing beef similar to stewing is braising. In this process, however, only a small amount of liquid is added to the saucepan, which does not entirely cover the meat. Instead of being simmered slowly on the fire, braised beef is also usually browned in a frying pan before being put in the oven to finish cooking.

Stewing in a very ancient method of preparing meat – especially beef – going as far back as prehistoric times. The term stewing comes from the Middle English *stewen*, meaning

A 1970s advertisement for Dinty Moore's beef stew, a popular item in the USA.

literally 'to bathe in a steam bath'. The word originates from the Old French *estuver*, a derivative of the Vulgar Latin term *extufare*, meaning 'to bathe'. Several examples of beef being slowly cooked in liquid can be found in the historical cookbooks of many nations and cultures around the world. In his *Histories*, Herodotus records that in the eighth century BC the Scythians – the term used by the ancient Greeks to refer to certain Iranian populations – were already known to 'put the flesh into an animal's paunch, mix water with it, and boil it like that over the bone fire'. Herodotus claimed that this rudimentary way of preparing stew allowed the 'bone to burn very well' and that 'the paunch easily' contained 'all the meat' once it had stripped off, so that 'in this way an ox' was 'ingeniously made to boil itself'. Other historical records also show that examples such as goulash (or *gulyàsleves*), a traditional Hungarian beef stew served over noodles, was already commonly eaten in the Magyar region in the ninth century, pre-dating the very existence of Hungary by several centuries. Guillaume Tirel's *Le Viandier* – the oldest French cookbook in existence, circulated in 1395 as a version of an earlier French cookery text – relates several recipes for beef stews and ragouts.

In modern times, a large number of beef stew recipes build up the culinary fibres of many international cuisines. Admirers of this particular cooking method are truly spoiled for choice. In Vietnam, for instance, *bo kho* is a traditional beef stew that is richly spiced and served with bread, rice or noodles. In the u.s., beef booyah is an elaborate beef stew that takes several days to prepare and is typical of the Upper Midwestern states. Booyah is especially cooked in 'booyah kettles', large-scale pots that were invented in the early 1900s by Clarence Rogers – also widely credited with the invention of booyah – that can hold multiple gallons of the stew. The name is thought to be an Anglicized amalgamation of the French *bouillir* (to boil) and *bouillon* (broth). Historically, booyah has been served in Midwestern states as a 'community dish', which is consumed collectively by the whole village during festivals and fundraising events.

The most well known incarnation of beef stew around the world, however, is perhaps beef bourguignon – also known as beef Burgundy or, most traditionally, *boeuf à la Bourguignonne*. The dish originates in the Burgundy region of France (La Bourgogne). The distinctive feature about this beef stew is that it is prepared with red wine, usually of the Burgundy variety, mixed with beef stock and then seasoned with onions, garlic and the traditionally French bouquet garni. Mushrooms are also added towards the end of cooking, in order to enhance the dish's already prominent earthy taste. In the American imagination, beef Bourguignon was popularized by renowned chef Julia Child, who made it one of her signature dishes.

Historically, beef bourguignon was part of the peasant cookbook of France. The rural legacy of the dish lies in its use of tough beef cuts such as chuck; the wine was arguably added to the stew in order to help tenderize the meat, which was naturally harder in texture than some of its more sought-after and sophisticated counterparts. In modern times, there has been a successful effort to refine the dish as an example of haute cuisine. A recipe for beef bourguignon appears in Auguste Escoffier's culinary textbook *Le Guide Culinaire* and offers instructions to prepare the dish that are still commonly followed around the world in order to maintain its original flavour. In even more recent times, the dish is thought of, outside of France, as a standard French dish, encapsulating all the charm and the sophistication of this particular European country.

Sous vide

Sous vide – French for 'under vacuum' – is another particular way of cooking beef that has been known for centuries. Another example of moist heat, the modern version of the method sees beef being cooked in sealed and airtight plastic bags. The bags are placed in water for a long period of time, sometimes as long as 72 hours, at the superficially determined temperature of 60°C (140°F). The intention behind this particular method is to ensure that the meat is cooked evenly on both the outside and the inside. Many sceptics of the method have termed it an unnecessarily sophisticated version of the old 'boil in the bag'. In reality, *sous vide* proves the perfect method for maintaining control in the kitchen. The typical tough nature of beef makes it an ideal candidate for undergoing the *sous vide* treatment, allowing it to stay juicy in spite of longer cooking times.

While *sous vide* as a precise technique may be a relatively new invention, the fundamental elements of the practice are known to be ancient. Many cultures – especially in central and Southeast Asia – have traditional beef-based dishes in which the meat is tightly wrapped in various artefacts and cooked slowly at a low temperature, maintaining moisture within the food. In written records, *sous vide* is first described as such by the physicist Sir Benjamin Thompson in 1799. While being treated as a common and somewhat unsophisticated way of preparing meat for centuries, *sous vide* was rediscovered in the late 1960s, when what is known as the 'modern era of *sous vide*' began. During this time, *sous vide* was used as an industrial preservation method that proved particularly effective with beef. French chef Georges Pralus for the Restaurant Troisgros officially adopted the method for cooking meat and put *sous vide* in the spotlight.

In industry terms, *sous vide* is also known as 'cryovacking', which literally describes putting food in plastic bags and vacuum packing. This particular term was coined by Bruno Goussault, a pioneer in developing the appropriate parameters and cooking times for the technique. In 1974, Goussault presented a study on the *sous vide* cooking of beef shoulder at an international frozen-foods conference in Strasbourg, France. He found that cooking the beef *sous vide* extended its shelf life to 60 days. Since then, *sous vide* has remained a standard cooking method for beef and other meats in restaurants worldwide.

The popularity of *sous vide* has re-emerged even on the home market in recent years thanks to the endorsement of renowned British chef Heston Blumenthal. He has been experimenting with the method since the late 1990s; his 'beef steak *sous vide*' gained a lot of attention in the British media and is praised as an example of culinary art that is as close to perfect as beef could ever be. On several occasions, Blumenthal has declared that *sous vide* will revolutionize the way people cook at home. *Sous vide*'s failure to enter the home market has been partially due to the expense involved in the method, as special boiling machines – manufactured by Supreme for decades – are necessary to achieve the intended results. Blumenthal, on the other hand, intends his new line of *sous vide* machines to be more affordable for the general public, carrying the assurance that a common piece of sirloin will be cooked to be so tender and juicy that guests will believe it is in fact beef fillet.

3
Raw and Cured

In a famous episode from the British television series *Mr Bean*, starring Rowan Atkinson, the title character goes to a sophisticated French restaurant to celebrate his birthday. After giving himself a birthday card, Mr Bean orders a posh-sounding dish from the menu. His anticipation for the culinary delights promised by the dish, however, quickly disappears as the order appears on the table: it is steak tartare, a dish of raw beef. Unable to admit to the waiter that he is unhappy with his order – as he was in fact expecting to receive a cooked steak – Mr Bean's reaction to the famous raw steak is nonetheless pure disgust. Its taste and texture cause poor Mr Bean to be repulsed by the very sight of it. He then proceeds, between one retching moment and the other, to cut up and hide pieces of the steak tartare in a variety of different places, including an ashtray, a sugar pot, a tiny vase and a hollowed-out bread roll.

More so than any other types of meat, beef can be enjoyed raw. Although the idea itself may turn the more delicate stomach, raw beef has been transformed into a delicacy in several countries. Towering among all renowned raw beef recipes across the globe is definitely Mr Bean's own choice, steak tartare, a dish made from minced or very finely chopped raw beef. The meat must be of the highest quality and for this reason filet mignon is usually the preferred cut. Tartare is often served with capers, chopped onions, a variety of seasonings – including Worcestershire sauce – and a raw egg yolk on top. The dish made its first ever appearance in French restaurants at the beginning of twentieth century. In those days, what we now generally call steak tartare was actually referred to as steak *à l'Americaine*. This dish consisted simply of raw beef, with no additional accompaniments or seasonings. The modern steak tartare originated from a later variation of steak *à l'Americaine*, when it was served with tartare sauce on the side. This incarnation of the dish first appeared in Auguste Escoffier's *Le Guide Culinaire* (1921 edition). Escoffier, however, does not mention the presence of egg yolk in this particular dish. With time, the clear distinction between steak tartare and steak *à l'Americaine* disappeared. In *Larousse Gastronomique* (1938 edition), steak tartare is clearly described as a dish of raw, finely chopped beef, served with a raw egg yolk. This incarnation does not mention tartare sauce at all.

The idea of serving beef raw is, of course, not only found in France. The propensity to eat beef raw can be found in several cuisines around the world, even historically pre-dating the appearance of steak tartare on French dinner tables. In Korean cuisine, for instance, *yukhoe* is a popular dish. '*Hoe*' refers collectively to a number of raw dishes in the country and *yukhoe* specifically is usually made from raw, ground beef which is then seasoned with spices or even sauces. Known in the industry as the 'Korean steak tartare' – a particular appellative that Korean chefs would probably refuse to acknowledge – *yukhoe* also uses the most tender parts of beef. Unlike in steak tartare, however, the beef for *yukhoe* is thinly julienned (instead of being finely chopped) and the fat is completely removed. The meat is usually mixed with soy sauce, oil, salt, sugar, garlic, sesame seeds and *bae* (a Korean pear); like in the most recent incarnations of steak tartare, a raw egg is also added on top of *yukhoe*.

Historically, the dish is said to have reached Korean shores from China in the late Goryeo period and became fashionable during the Joseon era. *Yukhoe* made its first written appearance in the late-nineteenth-century Korean cookbook *Siuijeonseo*, compiled by an anonymous cook. In this particular account, it is recommended for slices of raw beef to be washed several times in water to remove all traces of blood. After the beef is seasoned, *Siuijeonseo* also recommends for the *yukhoe* to be served with *chogochujang*, a specific dipping sauce made with chillies, sugar and vinegar.

Another dish of raw beef comes from Italy and is, of course, the famous carpaccio. This consists of thinly cut slices of beef, seasoned with olive oil, Parmigiano-Reggiano or Grana Padano shavings, lemon and rocket. The lemon juice is said to 'cook' the beef to some extent, mitigating its taste and texture. In recent years, mustard has been used by more experimental chefs as a seasoning, in order to counterbalance the acidity of the meat with a creamier, softer taste. According to culinary folklore, the dish originated at Harry's Bar in Venice, where it was first served to countess Amalia Nani Mocenigo by the bar owner Giuseppe Cipriani. The countess had allegedly been ordered by her doctor to consume only raw meat. Carpaccio was named after the fifteenth-century Italian painter Vittore Carpaccio, as Cipriani claimed that the colours of the dish reminded him of the palette commonly used by the Renaissance artist in his paintings. Although the history of the dish is more attributable to legend than actual historical fact, this does not affect the popularity of carpaccio itself, which still remains one of the most popular and distinguished ways to consume raw beef around the world.

The popular steak tartare.

Beef carpaccio, presented at a restaurant in Italy with the modern addition of mustard as a topping.

In Chile, *crudos* is a typical dish of raw beef mince served between slices of bread and seasoned with lemon juice, onion and a yoghurt-based sauce. In Ethiopia, the local cuisine includes *kifto*, a special dish of raw beef marinated in *mitmita*, a spicy chilli blend, and *niter kibbeh*, a clarified butter infused with spices and herbs. The term *kifto* – sometimes spelled *kefto* – derives from an ancient Ethio-Semitic root (k-f-t) meaning 'to mince'. An Eritrean variation of *kifto* is *gored gored*, where the raw beef is left unmarinated and is served cubed instead of minced.

Recently, health concerns have reduced the popularity of raw beef dishes in some parts of the world. Particularly in Western countries, the fear of contamination by parasites and bacteria – which have been found to live in raw meat – have turned the stomachs of many adventurous beef-eaters. *Taenia saginata* and *Toxoplasma gondii* are but two examples of harmful parasites that can fester in raw beef. Nonetheless, if basic hygienic rules are followed and methods of preparation monitored, the risk of contracting these parasites is very low. Even salmonella infections are known to be very rare if the raw beef is stored correctly and handled appropriately during preparation.

Overall, however, the popularity of raw beef does not seem to be completely threatened by widespread health concerns. Caution must be exercised, though. Raw beef makes for an extraordinary and almost surreal experience. Even to the most trained palates, the taste is peculiar, pungent and forceful. While the distinguished Carpaccio calls for admirers and camouflages its true, red-blooded nature underneath layers of lemon juice, rocket and Parmigiano-Reggiano, a candid steak tartare is not for everyone. Its raw honesty can be a difficult gift to accept.

In a similar fashion to its raw counterpart, cured beef takes many shapes and forms, including several types of flavouring and preservation processes that range from smoking to salting and pickling. Salt and sugar have been known historically to be two of the most widely used additions in the preservation of beef, especially in European regions. The process of preserving beef with salt, in particular, is known to be ancient, as a number of historical accounts from around the world testify to the practice being common among multiple cultures. Examples of dry-cured salted beef – which have evolved greatly over the centuries – can be located in Europe, Africa, South Asia and the Americas. Cured beef is appealing in concept as it allows the preservation of large quantities of meat for very long periods of time, permitting for a food source to be readily available even during periods of scarcity or poor weather conditions.

One of the most well-known types of salt-cured beef, known in several cultures around the world, is corned beef. The term 'corned' does not have any affinity with actual corn; indeed, many an inexperienced eater has expected a layer of corn around the beef and been rather disappointed at its absence. In this case, in fact, 'corned' derives from the Old English word for grain, which used to refer to anything that was round in shape. Where corned beef is concerned, the 'roundness' refers to the salt grains that are still used today in preparing and curing the meat.

In terms of written records, early references to dry-salted beef appear in the eleventh century. The historian Regina Sexton points out that a similar salted product is mentioned in *Aislinge Meic Con Glinne*, a Middle Irish tale of unknown authorship. The first mention of corned beef as such appears in Richard Burton's *Anatomy of Melancholy*, a text published in 1621: 'Beef a strong and hearty meat . . . for labouring men if ordered aright, corned, young, of an ox.' In modern times, 'corned beef' is used commonly and interchangeably to refer

A can of corned beef. The process of canning as a standard preservation method proved essential in establishing this product's popularity on an international scale.

to a number of cured beef varieties. Indeed, there are several ways in which what we call corned beef can be produced. The most traditional type of corned beef is a cured product dehydrated with grain salt, which maintains a firmer and drier texture for the meat and can be made with various and different cuts of beef. This product is usually served 'fresh' in delicatessen shops. The canned variety of corned beef, on the other hand, while still being prepared with grain salt, is known to have an oily and crumbly appearance and texture. In the UK, canned corned beef is also traditionally referred to as bully beef, a term derived from the French *boeuf bouilli*, meaning literally 'boiled beef'. These two types of corned beef still qualify as 'dry-cured products'.

Another variety of corned beef, however, can be wet-cured in strongly spiced brine, which allows the meat to preserve a suppler and tender texture. This pickled form of corned beef is particularly popular in North America, where brisket is the favourite cut to make the product. In the u.s., corned beef is still the main ingredient in what is known as the Reuben sandwich, a common lunchtime speciality consisting of corned beef, Swiss cheese and sauerkraut. Modern manufacturers of corned beef are known to include saltpetre in both the dry-curing salt and the brine in order to preserve the characteristically pink colour of the meat.

Corned beef is a historically charged variety of cured beef. Its own history, popularity and development are closely tied to the history of the uk, the u.s. and Ireland. Although the practice of salt-curing beef is ancient, the mass-scale production of corned beef is known to have started during the British Industrial Revolution. It was during this time that a lot of the farmland in Ireland was converted to pastures in order to accommodate cattle for the production of beef. Ireland was without a doubt the biggest producer of corned beef in the eighteenth century, supplying most of the meat for the Atlantic trade. The city of Cork had already earned itself a name as a beef-producing city in the seventeenth century; by 1668 Cork was responsible for half of the entire beef production of Ireland.

During the years of the Irish Famine (1740–1741), the cattle industry in Ireland – demanding large portions of the land and intensified to sustain the high demands for corned beef by the British Navy – contributed to, in parallel to the already poor weather conditions, preventing the raising of sustainable crops that could feed the Irish population. In *Beyond Beef*, Jeremy Rifkin points out that the 'British taste for beef had a devastating impact on the impoverished and disfranchised people of Ireland', as they were pushed off 'the Celtic grazing lands' and into 'small plots of marginal land'. In spite of the fact that Ireland was one of the biggest producers of beef for the British, the prohibitive cost of the meat forced the local Irish population to turn to less nourishing crops, cementing a long-lasting association between the Irish diet and the potato.

In the seventeenth and eighteenth centuries, it was not usual practice to distinguish between common and prized cuts when producing corned beef. Rather, the distinction was carried out according to the size and weight of the cattle, producing what was known as 'small beef', 'cargo beef' and 'best mess beef' – with the first being considered the worst quality and the last the best. The most desirable portions were usually the ones that were kept for English consumption either at home or in the colonies, while the less prized consignments were traded on the foreign market.

In the late eighteenth century, the development of canning as a way of containing and preserving meat transformed the production of corned beef into an international form of trade. Canned corned beef was officially distributed to the British Armed Forces in 1813 and proved a convenient source of nourishment due to its long lasting and unperishable nature. In the late nineteenth century, corned beef began to lose its role as a commodity for the British Royal Navy and Army; nonetheless its importance as an enduring source of food was greatly restored during the world wars. During the Second World War, in particular, corned beef was not only shipped to the British Armed Forces in Europe, but also became a staple ration of the civilian population. At this time, however, the beef consumed by the British mainly came from South America, with Uruguay and Argentina having become the biggest source of corned beef for the UK by 1943.

In the U.S. and Canada, corned beef – coupled with cabbage – is still the main ingredient in the culinary celebrations or St Patrick's Day. Historically, there is no association between St Patrick, corned beef and cabbage, but this does not deter the Irish-American community from consuming large quantities of the meat as part of the cultural and religious festivity. Indeed, corned beef and cabbage are not part of the national diet in Ireland. The closest dish that one can find is a traditional pairing of cabbage and bacon, testifying to the longstanding Irish preference for pork. The switch from pork to beef was probably due to the low prices of canned corned beef in the nineteenth century in America, which likely inspired the newly arrived Irish immigrants to develop a penchant for consuming the beef product. It is strange to think that the Irish were known to salt beef for the British for centuries, but did not actually begin to consume it as a staple food until the late 1800s when they emigrated to the New World.

In Eastern areas of the u.s. – such as New York City – the Jewish community have also been known to produce a kosher

A traditional North American St Patrick's Day feast of corned beef and cabbage.

salted beef, which has been sold in Jewish American delis centuries. Many disputes have taken place about the shared cultural and culinary heritage that both Irish and Jewish communities have in connection to corned beef in the U.S. In truth, the Jewish version of corned beef – usually served on rye bread – developed almost independently from its Irish counterpart. Both the Jewish and the Irish were known to produce dry-salted beef long before they met on the American shores of the Atlantic. The only connection between the two cultures, when it comes to beef, was the shared trade circles that both communities were known to rely on when obtaining the meat.

Corned beef, however, is but one example of how beef can be cured and made available for consumption over periods of time. The techniques for curing beef are varied and produce similar, yet differing, products. Bresaola, for instance, is a type of air-dried, salted beef originating from the Valtellina region of Northern Italy. The meat is aged for at least three months until it becomes hard and assumes its characteristic dark red colouring. Although bresaola can be made from various cuts of beef, including underloin, loin and haunch, legs of beef are usually preferred for the task.

The origin of the name bresaola is uncertain. Some believe the term derives from '*sala come brisa*', a reference to the salting process that is used to preserve the meat. Others claim that it derives from *brasa*, a local dialect word used in reference to the braces or 'embers' employed in the heat chambers during the drying phase. The first historical testimonies of bresaola can be found in Italian records from the fifteenth century. Nonetheless, it is likely that a meat similar to bresaola had been known to the area of Valtellina for much longer before that, as salting and drying was the favourite method used by local families to preserve their meats. Legend

it that, for centuries, bresaola was particularly favoured
y local smugglers, who – thanks to the cured beef – had a
ong-lasting source of food while travelling across the moun-
tains into Switzerland in journeys lasting weeks at a time.

Bresaola is granted a special status in the European Union
as a PGI product (or 'Protected Geographical Indication'). Its
production in Italy is safeguarded by Consorzio Bresaola
della Valtellina, which ensures that the meat is prepared and
marketed in the approved manner. The consortium regularly
issues specific guidelines that the producers must abide by in
order for their finished product to be granted the name of
'*bresaola della Valtellina*'. The consortium calls specifically for the
trimming – where the fat is completely removed from the meat
– and subsequent dry-salting of the beef. The meat is carefully
covered with salt, which contains flavourings such as sugar
and spices. While working within the consortium's guidelines,
each producer is allowed to add particular flavourings, such
as wine, juniper berries, cinnamon and nutmeg, in order to
create a specific taste that is particular to their own production.

There are several steps that must be followed in order
to create proper *bresaola della Valtellina*. During the salting
process, the beef is rubbed thoroughly so that the salt mixture can penetrate deeply below the surface. The beef is then
pressed and wrapped in casings – which can be either natural,
such as the cow's intestines, or artificial – and readied for the
drying process. The drying is done in boxes of low humidity
with a temperature that usually ranges between 20°C and 30°C
(68°F and 86°F). During this process, the beef is quickly
drained of its moisture, losing more than 40 per cent of its
original weight. In the final process of making bresaola, the
beef is allowed to cool in areas where natural air exchange
takes place. This final drying stage must last for at least four
weeks. Afterwards, bresaola is usually served in thin slices so

that it can be sprinkled with olive oil and black peppe[r] manner not too dissimilar to the raw dish of carpaccio. taste, however, is completely different to that of raw be[ef] bresaola is sweet-flavoured with a smoky aroma.

Cured beef, however, is not only a prerogative of European food makers. A good example of this is biltong, a dry-cured meat that originates in South Africa. It has traditionally been made with a variety of meats, ranging from beef to game. Nonetheless, beef is now one of the most common and primary ingredients, to the extent that the appellative 'beef biltong' has become redundant. The finest cuts are used to make biltong, including sirloin and fillet steak. The name 'biltong' is a composite of the Dutch words *bil* (rump) and *tong* (strip). Biltong, therefore, means literally 'strip of meat'. Its name is mirrored in the meat's distinctive shape – it is often seen hanging in strips in various butchers' shops in South Africa.

When it comes to shaping the history of biltong, local African folklore has it that when migrating tribesmen were herding their stock, they would place strips of meat under the saddles of their horses. The chafing was said to tenderize the meat, while the saddle was meant to flavour the beef. This story, although picturesque, is enough to make culinary adventurers queasy and it is a true relief that the biltong-making industry has decided to leave its traditional tenderizing and salting methods behind. As it is known today, biltong owes a lot of its composition, texture and flavour to the traditions of the Dutch pioneers in South Africa – the Voortrekkers – who were known to sun-dry their meat during their travels across the subcontinent. The drying, of course, was intended to preserve the meat for longer periods of time. The basic mixture used to season biltong was – and still is today – a remarkable blend of salt, vinegar, coriander and spices. These

A platter of sliced *bresaola della Valtellina*.

were abundant in what was known in the nineteenth century as Cape Colony, thanks to its geographical position on the East Indian route.

Today biltong is widely consumed not only in South Africa, but also in several countries around the world. Currently, the biggest producers of the cured beef outside of the African subcontinent are Germany and New Zealand. In the latter, the impact of substantial immigration from South Africa has transformed biltong into one of the most widely known dry beef products in the country, so that it can be commonly found in all food shops and supermarkets.

In the Americas, cured beef has found one of its most popular incarnations in jerky. This particular type of dried meat is made from very lean beef which is trimmed of all fat and dried to preserve it. The process to make beef jerky is relatively simple, since all that is needed is a constant heat source and a good supply of salt, which will inhibit the growth of bacteria and preserve the meat. Modern manufacturing methods

Biltong at a butcher's shop in Johannesburg.

have the beef marinated in a seasoned liquid or powder, and then dehydrated – or sometimes smoked, as was preferred in older times – with a low heat that usually hovers around the 70°C (158°F) mark. Some makers of jerky, especially in areas such as Texas, prefer to use the 'traditional' method of preparation, simply salting the beef slices thoroughly and allowing it to sun-dry slowly. The result of both modern and traditional methods is a salty, smoky product which can be easily consumed as a snack and stored for several months. Unlike bresaola, the drying process in jerky happens quickly and, in present-day factories, it takes place in large ovens made with insulated panels, rather than in drying chambers. On occasions, sweet varieties of jerky can be produced by adding sugar to the marinating rub. This sweet variety puts jerky in stark contrast with other dry beef varieties such as biltong, where salt and vinegar (rather than sugar) are used to inhibit bacterial growth and ensure preservation of the meat.

The name 'jerky' is a corruption of the Spanish term *charqui*, which in itself was derived from *ch'arki*, a common word in the Quechuan language – spoken by the Incas and their descendants – meaning literally 'burnt meat'. The history of jerky is open to debate. There is a tendency to believe that Native Central American tribes made several variations of jerky for thousands of years. The first written record of jerky being produced in the Americas can be found in Spanish records from the 1500s, in which the Quechuan people are reported to consume large quantities of dry meat. When European explorers arrived in the New World, they found that the native tribes could preserve meat for long periods of time thanks to specific drying processes. They were immediately intrigued by the possibility of having meat that would not spoil and could be transported easily on their travels. The explorers gained knowledge of how to cure and prepare the meat and how to season and dry it in order to transform it into jerky. Jerky, however, reached the height of its popularity in the eighteenth century, during the years of the North American expansion. Once again, colonization and land discovery was at the heart of dry beef's success in several communities, as its ability to be transported for days, if not months, without spoiling made it the perfect food fo[r] and adventurous explorers.

As the industrial age boomed in North America, the p[op]ularity of beef jerky did not diminish and the meat bega[n] to be mass-produced. Jerky, of course, is not made only with beef, as other popular incarnations include buffalo jerky, venison jerky and, more recently, ostrich jerky. However, the widespread presence of cattle and cheaper prices of beef have allowed beef jerky to become one of the most common and widely available types of cured beef one can find in North America. Today, jerky is consumed in large quantities by many populations around the world, its uncompromising taste still carrying a touch of the adventurous life on the pioneer trail.

4
A Cut Above

Before it is cooked or prepared for consumption, beef must first be divided into primal cuts. These are large pieces of meat which are originally separated from the carcass during the initial stages of butchering. Subsequent sections of beef – such as steak – are cut from these large pieces of meat. One should not be tempted to think that both the primal and secondary division of beef is simply a matter of practicality and common sense. Culture and social organization have a strong impact on how beef is cut in different countries and geographical areas. The Koreans and the Bodi people in Africa are known to be the most thorough and specific in dividing beef for consumption. The Bodi people are known to have 51 cuts of beef, while the Koreans go as far as separating the meat into an amazing number of 120 cuts. These divisions are not only connected to the specific culinary uses that are intended for the beef, but are also reliant on ritual associations that are fundamental to the practice of butchering cattle around the world.

In Western countries, the principal ways of cutting beef are divided into American and British cuts. Although these are not universal in any way, they can be used as a starting point to unravel how cuts of beef are differentiated and prepared. In

A colour illustration from *Webster's Illustrated Dictionary* (1920).

American primal cuts, the carcass is split along its axis sym-metrically into 'halves', then divided across into front and back quarters – what are also known as forequarters and hind-quarters. Forequarters cuts include the chuck, the rib, the shank and the plate. The chuck is usually the source of bone-in steaks and boneless clod steaks and roasts. The first references to 'chuck' as a cut of beef appear in sixteenth-century English cooking manuals, although the origin of the term is uncertain.

The rib contains the short ribs, the prime rib and rib eye steaks. The plate is a section found below the ribs used prim-arily for pot roasting. A full slab of short ribs is usually 25 square centimetres (4 square inches) and 7 to 12 centimetres (4 to 5 inches) thick. They can also be cut into boneless steaks, although these must not be confused with 'boneless country-style beef ribs', another cut that was recently introduced in the U.S. as a cheaper alternative to rib steak. The rib eye steak – also known as 'Scotch fillet' in New Zealand and Australia – is mainly composed of *Longissimus dorsi* muscle on the carcass. The rib eye is the base for the famous 'Delmonico steak', a particular way of preparing beef meat that was made popu-lar by the renowned Delmonico's Steakhouse Restaurant in New York City in the mid-nineteenth century. In spite of the fact that the rib eye has been commonly associated with the Delmonico steak, there have been many controversies over the years surrounding which cut would have originally been used. Many sources claim to have proof on the matter and it is estimated that up to eight cuts could have qualified as the original cut for the world-famous steak. These ranged from rib eye steak (boneless and with bone) to sirloin. The main controversy was centred on whether Delmonico steak should be boneless or not. Historically speaking, the two principal chefs that were working at Delmonico's in the 1840s and 1850s – Alessandro Filippini and Charles Ranhofer – both wrote

Delmonico steak, as served at the restaurant of the same name in New York.

recipe books citing the Delmonico steak as a boneless cut of beef, whether sirloin or rib eye. In the twenty-first century, the controversy around Delmonico steak seems to have settled, so that the name has been widely used as a fancy term for rib eye steak, whether broiled, grilled or fried.

Brisket, on the other hand, is a cut that is used primarily in the West for barbecues or for making corned beef. This does not tend to be the tendency in Asia, however, where brisket is used primarily for stews. A famous Chinese dish employing this particular cut is five-spice beef, a preparation method made famous in the U.S. by celebrity chef, talk-show host and television personality Rachael Ray. As a cut, the shank is also used mainly for stews and soups. As this is the part of the animal that does most of the work, it tends to be cooked mainly through moist heat. It is not a surprise, then, that beef shanks are often the main ingredients in dishes such as Irish stew or beef bourguignon.

Hindquarters on the carcass of beef include loin, round and flank. The round is a relatively lean cut of beef, mainly used for round steak and particularly popular in Argentina, Brazil and Germany; in the latter, round steak is the main ingredient in *rinderbraten*, a spiced beef dish stuffed with pork fat. A particular variation of *rinderbraten* was exported to the U.S. in 1961 by William Jacobs, a German meatpacker originally from Wittenberg, and found its New World incarnation in spiced round, a beef dish once very common as a Sunday meal in the Nashville area.

The loin comprises three principal sub-primal cuts: the short loin, the sirloin and the tenderloin. The short loin forms the basis for T-bone and porterhouse steaks; if cut boneless, this section of beef is used as strip steak, and is also known as New York strip. The name 'porterhouse' is uncertain in origin, although two likely – and utterly differing – stories have been circulated over the years. One account claims that the steak originated in historic Midway, Kentucky, a popular dish at the Porter House, an inn that operated between 1864 and 1901. Another source insists that porterhouse steak has its origins in New York City, where this cut of beef was first served at Martin Morrison's Porter House in 1814. In spite of the disagreeing sources in existence, however, the general consensus is that porterhouse steak probably originated in the nineteenth century from some form of 'porter house', a tavern that served food. Rather than being named after the form of establishment in which it was served, it is believed that porterhouse steak took its name from 'porter', a popular ale beverage served at these particular taverns.

T-bone, on the other hand, first appeared on menus in the U.S. in 1916. The cut is named after the bone section that runs down the lumbar vertebrae, surrounding the spinal muscle and forming a distinctive 'T' shape. T-bone is mostly suited for fast cooking methods that rely on dry heat. In Italy, a world-famous way of cooking T-bone steak is *bistecca alla Fiorentina* (steak 'Florentine style'). For this dish, the beef is usually taken either from the Maremma or Chianina cattle, breeds that are popular and widespread in the Tuscan region of Italy. In recent years, porterhouse steak has also been used for this dish, although T-bone remains the favourite cut. The typical *bistecca alla Fiorentina* is 2–5 centimetres (1–2 inches) thick, depending not only on availability but also on the preference of the eater. This steak is not only thickly cut, but also very large in size. The *bistecca* is usually grilled over a charcoal fire and seasoned with salt. It is invariably served extremely rare and, in virtue

Prime cut of beef fillet, prepared with mushrooms.

Bistecca alla Fiorentina as served in Florence. The thickness of the steak, which has made the dish famous all over the world, is clearly visible here.

of its size, is often intended to be shared between two people. During the years of the 'mad cow' scare in the 1990s, *bistecca alla Fiorentina* was banned from restaurants in Italy and Europe, only to return to the scene in 2001 to the welcoming roar of its avid fans.

British primal cuts are somewhat similar in concept to American cuts. Indeed, many terms of reference are used to describe the same parts of the carcass. Nonetheless, British cuts tend to be more numerous and more specific in their sub-divisions. The front of the carcass is usually divided into neck, chuck and blade and clod. These cuts tend to be tougher and are traditionally used in stews or braised dishes. The rib and leg areas are divided into fore rib, thin rib, brisket and shin. The brisket cut within the British system is much smaller and thinner than its American counterpart, and elongates towards the belly of the animal rather than being located strictly above the leg. The mid-section of the carcass is divided into sirloin and flank. The British sirloin primal cut is once again much smaller than the American one and is the section from which the fillet is derived; this sub-cut is usually put aside for grilling or frying by virtue of its natural tenderness. The back quarters of the carcass are instead divided into rump, silverside, top-side, thick flank and leg. Rump steaks are a rough equivalent to round steak in the American system, while top side, silverside and thick flank work best for roasting. The leg, forming the base for braising steak, makes the perfect ingredient in stews and casseroles.

In spite of the general impact of American and British cuts, one should not think that these form the only divisions for beef. In France, for instance, it is possible to find a large selection of cuts that are cheaper or most expensive according to their tenderness and intended use. These include *bavette* – a cheap undercut that comes from the skirt of the animal

Raw beef steaks, ready to be sold at a butcher's shop in England.

Grilled beef tongue. The cut is presented here as part of a fusion dish, incorporating ingredients from Western and Eastern cuisines.

and is usually textured with muscle fibres – and *aloyau*, a sub-cut roughly equivalent to British sirloin. French cuts of beef also tend to include beef tongue, *langue de boeuf*. This cut, however, is not exclusive to French cuisine. Historical records show that beef tongue has been consumed by humans for centuries, its popularity beginning at the dawn of civilization when Palaeolithic hunters were known to favour the fatty parts of the carcass as they provided a higher caloric intake – beef tongue is 75 per cent fat. As a cut, it is a popular ingredient within several cultures. Belgium, Mexico, Germany and Portugal are but a few countries that have beef tongue as a principal cut in their culinary repertoire.

Even in America, while this particular cut has now lost some of its favour among buyers, beef tongue is known to have been a popular choice for centuries, especially as filler for sandwiches. Particularly in the nineteenth century, American cookbooks were crowded with luncheon recipes that featured beef tongue as a main ingredient. Mrs Webster's *The Improved Housewife* (1844) offers a simple recipe for a quick and tasty sandwich, comprising of 'slices of biscuit', buttered and filled with 'a very thin slice of tongue'. *Mrs Cowan's American Ladies' Cookery Book* (1866) gives boiled tongue as a versatile ingredient in summer luncheons, ideally served with buttered bread and mustard. In 1942, American cook Ethel X. Pastor also praised the qualities of beef tongue in her *Wartime Entertaining*, listing her dish of 'Sliced Sweet and Sour Tongue' as an absolutely delicious addition to any dinner party. Nonetheless, hope is not lost for modern American connoisseurs as beef tongue has made a recent triumphant return in the U.S. as part of the popular tongue toast, an open-faced sandwich commonly served for breakfast and lunch in restaurants and hotels.

Ageing

Preparation, however, takes place long before the beef is even cut into steak and roasts. Cooking and eating are but the final step in the process that allows the meat to be ready for human consumption. Once the animal has been slaughtered, its flesh has to be put through scrupulous steps. The newly butchered meat has the tendency to be tough and still strongly held together by its connective tissues. In order for the meat to tenderize, the beef is usually put through a rigorous ageing process. This is done in order to break down the muscular fibres that would otherwise be extremely hard to chew. Beef can be aged through either dry or wet processes. Dry-ageing relies on the meat being hung and rested in a large cooler for a period of time. It is expensive, as it is time-consuming, taking up to 28 days to complete, and is usually reserved for larger pieces of beef and more highly prized cuts. Dry-ageing is usually a prerogative of beef that is purchased in expensive restaurants and steakhouses. Wet-ageing, on the other hand, is a much quicker process that is carried out in a vacuum-sealed bag. This is the most common method of ageing beef, especially in the U.S. and the UK, since it is relatively inexpensive. Most of the beef that can now be purchased in butcher shops in the West has been wet-aged. The taste of the beef, of course, is highly dependent on its ageing process and dry-ageing is without a doubt a more efficient way of tenderizing the meat and bringing out its most flavoursome qualities.

Chaim Soutine, *Carcass of Beef*, 1925, oil on canvas.

5
The Imagination of Beef

To claim that beef figures prominently as an imagistic medium in literature and art would be an outlandish statement. Nonetheless, even if it has not always taken the most central place in cultural forms throughout history, beef has played an important part in externalizing human fears and desires about their lives and conditions. There is no doubt that over the centuries beef has gained many cultural and social associations which art, literature and (in more recent years) films have helped to establish and maintain.

The impact of beef and cattle are evident in cultural organization not only in terms of economy and culinary preference, but also in linguistic terms. The English language, in particular, has many expressions containing the term 'beef' as a reference; the examples can be wide and disparate. When having arguments or complaining, people are said to 'have a beef'. 'To cry beef' is to give alarm and 'to beef up' something is to make it stronger and more effective. When someone is particularly well-built and muscled, the expression 'beefy' is widely common and 'beefcake' is a term used to denote a semi-nude or nude male body, especially in the body-building world. The appearance and reputation of beef as a strong and plentiful meat have clearly had a sizeable impact on the way in which

Aurochs found on the Forneau-du-Diable rock in Bourdeilles, France.

this particular food has entered and conquered common expression and idioms.

Art offers, perhaps, some of the greatest examples of how beef can be represented metaphorically. Indeed, beef – or at least cattle – was the subject of the earliest pieces of art produced by the human race. Aurochs are depicted in several Palaeolithic cave paintings from Europe and ancient Mesopotamia. The most famous of these are probably the ones found in Lascaux and Livernon in France. The hunting scenes portrayed in these paintings give us an insight into how important beef and beef consumption was to the lives of early men.

As humanity developed, beef remained a recurrent subject in paintings and frescoes, even if the meat itself was often a secondary agent in the picture, with the activities of people around it – usually hunting, cooking or eating – gaining centre stage. During the Renaissance, scenes depicting slaughtered cows were common, especially when the subject of the painting had a biblical connection. The parable of the prodigal son often received particular attention in this sense, with the carcass of beef – a symbol of celebration and wealth – functioning as a representation of the father's happiness upon his son's return home. An example of this is the famous engraving by Philips Galle depicting the carcass of beef being prepared for the upcoming banquet, while people are dancing and celebrating around it.

Beef carcasses in art often functioned as a reminder of emotion for humanity. While beef could represent joy and happiness, it could also be a reminder of death, a *memento mori* made of meat. Martin Van Cleve's *The Slaughtered Ox* (1566) is one of the first paintings to place the beef carcass at the centre of the image. The beef is hanging from the ceiling and ready to be rested; around it, the slaughterhouse workers enjoy an earned moment of rest, while children play in the background, blowing bubbles out of the cow's bladder (a common toy at the time). The beef carcass is uncompromising and confronting, probably functioning as a reminder of the frailty of life.

Almost a century later, in 1655, Rembrandt Harmenszoon van Rijn painted a small picture of a slaughtered ox. The beef carcass is the subject of the picture and hangs in a small, badly lit room; the ox is beheaded and skinned, and the organs and hooves have already been removed from the carcass. There are no human activities being performed in the painting, the only true remnants of human life within the room being the beef, as a reminder of the slaughtering which clearly occurred at some point. For lack of a better word, the painting can be described as eerie. The atmosphere is gloomy, with the light coming from unknown source. The room depicted is empty but for the beef, and the absence of other major elements add to its mystery. The *memento mori* motif – 'Remember that you must die' – is particularly unavoidable in this piece.

Rembrandt's *Carcass of Beef*, one of his later versions of the original painting from 1655, oil on canvas.

On the literary front, Lord Byron in particular showed a penchant for discussing beef in his poetry, often choosing curious ways to introduce the meat. In his satirical epic poem *Don Juan* (1824), for instance, Byron praises beef as a great ally when travelling at sea:

> The best of remedies is a beef-steak
> Against sea-sickness: try it, sir, before
> You sneer, and I assure you this is true,
> For I have found it answer – so may you.

In terms of novels, however, Charles Dickens wins the culinary prize for his delightful descriptions of Victorian breakfast, lunch and dinner, in which beef figures on almost every occasion. Dickens speaks fondly of a 'jolly round of beef' in *Barnaby Rudge* (1841) and of 'beef-steak puddings' in *Martin Chuzzlewit* (1844). Picnics centred on beef delights are also given particular attention in *The Pickwick Papers* (1837), with 'cold beef' and 'cold tongue' appearing as primary presences. In *Great Expectations* (1861), 'roast beef' is presented as the ideal meal to be proudly consumed with a pint of ale and plum pudding. Plentiful descriptions of 'boiled beef' also pepper the pages of Dickens's other works. In truth, Dickens gives us an accurate insight into the importance of beef in the British diet, ascribing to beef itself the ability to make a celebration out of every meal.

The imagistic connection between food and nationality is no more prominent in history than when it comes to the close love affair that the British have with beef. In historical terms, beef did not become figuratively associated with England until the eighteenth century, but the connection between the two was definitely known before then. In his *Compendyous Regyment, or a Dyetary of Health* (1542), Andrew Boorde clearly states that 'beef is a good meate for an Englyssman'. Shakespeare's most patriotic play, *Henry V* (*c.* 1599), confirms that already in the sixteenth century the English liked to think of themselves as a proud, beef-eating people. In Act III, Scene 7, the French – on the eve of the battle of Agincourt – scorn the English love for the meat; planning their strategy for battle, the Duke of Orleans comments that victory for France will be assured, since the English troops are 'shrewdly out of beef' and therefore unable to fight. It is particularly ironic that the French words are spoken on the eve of one of England's greatest military victories. Clearly, Shakespeare did have a sense of patriotic humour, even if of the culinary variety.

In the eighteenth century, beef emerged as a central presence in English patriotic songs and propaganda. Perhaps the most famous within this group is Henry Fielding's ballad

William Hogarth, *The Gate of Calais, or O The Roast Beef of Old England*, 1749, engraving.

'The Roast Beef of Old England', performed in 1731 as part of his play the *Grub-Street Opera*. Fielding uses beef as a metaphorical representation of the worth of England, which was mighty and great in older times. Beef also represents the wealth of traditional and reactionary beliefs:

> When mighty roast was the Englishman's food
> It ennobl'd our veins and enriched our blood
> Our soldiers were brave and our courtiers were good
> Oh! The roast beef of Old England, and Old English
>   roast beef.

The unwelcome foreign influence on British ideals is represented in culinary terms as well, with foreign food 'invading' the once magnificent country. The French, in particular, are pictured as the worst influence, with their flimsy 'ragouts' distracting good English men from their purpose and strength. In modern times, Fielding's 'The Roast Beef of Old England' maintains its evocative power and the tune is played at formal dinners both by the British Royal Navy and the United States Navy Bands whenever beef is presented.

Beef also played an important role in British satirical vignettes, mirroring both the cultural battle between the French and the English and widely commenting on the general political situation in Europe. William Hogarth's painting *The Gate of Calais, or O The Roast Beef of Old England* (1748) has beef as the central metaphor to encompass instances of English xenophobia. The picture borrowed its title from Fielding's patriotic ballad. Handling images with incredible dexterity, Hogarth transforms an apparently simple meaty foodstuff into a powerful symbol. The scene is organized around the gate itself – famously built by the English – where a servant carries a glorious hunk of English beef, which is put in stark contrast to a measly pot of French soup. The beef acts as a central point around which stereotypical figures of the time are grouped, such as a soldier, a friar and a free painter. The beef clearly represents the plentiful nature of England, well-satiated and faithful to tradition. The focus on the English meat reveals the inferiority of the French, who – being fed on light soup and, clearly, progressive ideals – are hungry both physically and psychologically as tyranny proves a depriving force. Beef acts as the ideal satiric medium to manipulate single stereotypes, in order to move from the institutional to the national level.

The cultural association between beef and liberal ideas was even honoured in Britain with the establishment of the Sublime Society of Beef Steaks in 1735. The club was founded by Hogarth himself and concerned itself primarily with organizing dinners for exclusive male guests and members. The diners would be consuming large quantities of beef and, with appropriate patriotic flair, discuss issues such as liberty and prosperity. The concepts largely attracted Whig sympathizers; notable members over the years included John Wilkes and Samuel Johnson. The society soon became celebrated as a patriotic group associated with the greatest men in the country; in 1785, the popularity of the society reached royal ears and even George IV – then the Prince of Wales – joined enthusiastically. In its stead as prized meat and patriotic symbol, beef maintained its place as a symbol of affluence, greatness and, of course, unremorseful patriarchy.

In the years after the French Revolution, the uses of beef as a proper British symbol reached their satirical zenith. These were the years when John Bull, a national personification of England, began to make a steady appearance in political cartoons and graphic works. In his earliest incarnations – originating in 1712 – John Bull was actually portrayed as a humanoid bull. In later works, and towards the end of the

James Gillray, *John Bull Triumphant*, 1780, coloured lithograph.

century, he was usually depicted as a stout, middle-aged man, commonly wearing a Union Jack waistcoat. One of the most significant characteristics of John Bull – aside from his virility, stubbornness and constant dislike of anything foreign, especially French – is that he is an avid beef eater. Some artists were known to use the figure of John Bull as a national emblem in caricatures of political situations, depicting particularly the contrast between post-Revolution France and Britain. A major exponent of this group was James Gillray, who amply used John Bull and his beef-eating in his satirical sketches. A famous example of Gillray's beef satire is *French Liberty, British Slavery* (1792). The picture depicts both a Frenchman and an Englishman consuming their stereotypical meals. The Frenchman – a ragged and emaciated *sans-culotte* – eats his meagre dinner of green onions, praising France's monarchy-free status. The Englishman, on the other hand, is depicted as grossly fat and is carving a large piece of roast beef. In spite of the fact that the John Bull character continues to complain about the 'ministry' and the 'taxes' in England, it is clear to the viewer that Gillray means to praise Britain, showing the living conditions in this country to be superior to those of France, where ideals of liberty obscure the meagre living conditions of its population.

The strong positive association between England and beef continued to remain robust during the nineteenth and twentieth centuries. This connection was known and appreciated both in Britain and on the foreign scene. In Erik Geijer's *Impressions of England, 1809–1810*, the Englishmen are described as 'patriots', whose stomachs seem to 'feel for the native land'. Geijer comments that Englishmen sit contentedly 'at their dinner-table, busy with their roast beef in as quiet and proud felicity as if they felt the whole worth of their favoured island on their tongues'. In the 1800s, prized breeds of cattle were also developed in Britain and beef became one of the country's greatest exports. Towards the end of the nineteenth century, beef was also established in England as traditional

James Gillray, *French Liberty, British Slavery*, 1792, hand-coloured etching.

A First World War advert for Bovril, laden with obvious beef propaganda.

Christmas fare, and 'Christmas beef' also came to represent the importance of the family unit for the country's stability. When the First World War hit, beef became emblematic of the war effort, as this particular meat was part of the rations sent to the troops at the front. It was also during this time that the figure of the beef-eating John Bull was resurrected

Promotional poster for the movie *City Slickers* (1991).

as a propagandist symbol, encompassing a disdain for Germany that reached its apogee during the years of the Second World War.

It is not just in England that beef and the cattle industry maintain a certain romanticized quality. As the gauchos of Argentina gaze into the stars at night, so do the cowboys in the u.s. This particular figure still manages to exercise its dreamy magic on the American population. In the film *City Slickers* (1991), for instance, the cattle industry is surrounded by a layer of wistful expectations, as a group of city-dwelling holiday makers – captained by Billy Crystal – take a trip herding cattle across the desert. As they dream of starry nights and camp-fires, the men's romantic vision of the roaming cowboy is put to the test as they realize not only that the life of the cattle herder is not easy and relaxed but also that beef – which has a tacit presence throughout the movie – is the result of their cattle herding, at the expense of the cows. The thought of dead cows and slaughterhouses is so strong that Crystal's character, Mitch, even refuses to leave behind Norman – the calf he helped to birth on his herding trip – turning him into an unlikely family pet. In the end, however, the longstanding loyalty towards the cattle industry takes over and a sense of American pride drowns out any animal-orientated thoughts that might destroy one of the most beloved fantasies the country holds.

Popular culture is undoubtedly tuned in to the ways of beef, providing many instances for discussion and reference. Cartoons and children's shows have incorporated the presence of beef over the years, ranging from Jiggs's passion for beef and cabbage to Desperate Dan's enormous cow pie and J. Wellington Wimpy's love for hamburgers. The latter loved burgers so much that he was even the inspiration for the name of the Wimpy burger restaurants, an American chain which was founded in the 1930s. *The Simpsons*, *Futurama*, *Family Guy* and *American Dad* are but a few of the several animated series aimed at adults that have featured beef in many situations, tackling important issues such as vegetarianism and beef hormone use in the cattle industry, often through a light-hearted but poignant perspective. It is hard to ignore the value of the episode of *The Simpsons*' entitled 'Bright Lights, Beef Jerky' as a pointed critique of commercialized life in contemporary societies. In the world of Japanese anime, beef takes a special role in Hayato Date's *Naruto*, where the title character consumes large quantities of his famous beef ramen every time he wins a battle.

In recent years, the controversies surrounding beef have indeed managed to add a layer of prohibitive and outrageous value to the artistic uses of this meat. In September 2010, American pop star Lady Gaga 'shocked' the eyes of the world when she attended the MTV Music Awards ceremony in Los Angeles dressed in pieces of bright red raw beef, arranged on her body to form a suitable outfit. Gaga's 'beef dress' was complemented by an array of equally meaty accessories; she appeared on the red carpet complete with a beefsteak hat and red marbled steak boots. To complete her escapade into a very literal interpretation of the beef imagination, Lady Gaga also posed naked for *Vogue Hommes Japan* with nothing but beef steak covering her modesty. Needless to say, Gaga's provocative outfits generated the attention she was no doubt interested in, and the outrage of animal rights and humanitarian groups alike.

There is no doubting, however, that beef makes its most unavoidable appearance in contemporary art forms – including films, animations and novels – through the medium of the burger. The presence of the burger as both a cultural and national icon, especially when it comes to the U.S., has been amply explored in a variety of media, with an impressive number of books and articles (both academic and popular in nature) being published on the subject in recent years.

Advertising has also played an important part in emphasizing the imagistic value of beef not only as food, but also as a cultural medium. 'Eat Mor Chikin' is the famous slogan of fast food chain Chick-fil-A. The company opened its first freestanding store in 1986 and has been using the famous phrase in its advertising campaigns since the early 1990s. The adverts themselves usually feature cows holding signs enticing

Lady Gaga wearing one of her beef outfits.

The famous advertising campaign for Chick-fil-A, created in 1995.

customers to 'eat more chicken'. According to Chick-fil-A's advertising folklore, the cows have united against the consumption of beef, in an effort to reform American food habits. Over the years, the cows have received a lot of attention as a popular culture icon – especially on the Internet – and are widely known even outside of the u.s. The 'Eat Mor Chikin' ads were momentarily suspended in 2003 in the wake of bse, in order to show sensitivity (or so it was claimed) to the difficulties experienced by the cattle industry. The cows made a triumphant return to the advertising scene in 2004.

Beef, however, finds its most popular advertising connection in the incredibly famous Wendy's campaign focused on the catchphrase 'Where's the Beef?' The catchphrase made its debut in a 1984 ad, in which actress Clara Peller visits a Wendy's competitor and receives a huge bread bun containing a tiny beef patty. Peller reacts with outrage and anger to

the small burger and (famously) exclaims 'Where's the .
The advert found huge success in the industry and the ca
phrase quickly transcended its commercial domain. To th
day, the slogan is used commonly in the U.S. and Canada as an
all-purpose phrase used when questioning the substance or
quality of a product or idea. Beef, it would seem, does not
disappoint, especially when it comes down to being an apt
medium of communication.

6
The Beef Controversies

Any of us would kill a cow, rather than not have beef.
Samuel Johnson

There is no way around it: if you want to eat beef, you've got to kill some cows. Slaughterhouses are the middle step of the beef industry, and yet represent the most significant stage in the creation of meat, the moment when the animal ceases to be a cow and becomes 'beef'. There is a certain sense of detachment in the Western world about the process that transforms a living and breathing animal into dead matter fit for consumption. Nonetheless, slaughterhouses and slaughtering methods have often been the centre of political controversies and cultural disputes.

Most countries have civil laws regulating the slaughtering process. In the u.s., for instance, the Humane Slaughter Act – outlined in 1958 – required all cattle to be unconscious before they are shackled and hoisted up on the slaughtering line. Unfortunately, the standards and regulations surrounding the slaughtering process vary significantly around the world. In several areas of the world, the slaughter of cows is regulated mainly by tradition and custom, rather than civil law. In Westernized countries, where slaughter is carried out

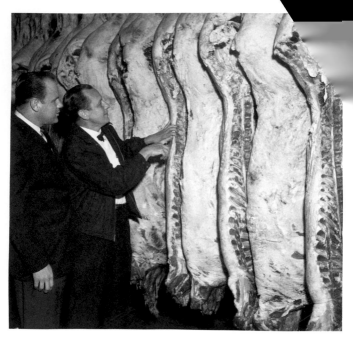

Beef carcasses being inspected in Texas in 1966.

in a mechanized fashion, the cows reach their final destination in the slaughterhouse through repetitive factory processes that usually rely on exsanguination – bleeding to death – to kill the animal. Rumours that cows are allowed to suffer unnecessarily in the slaughtering process have attracted the attention of several provocative animal welfare groups, such as the Humane Farming Association. In her book *Slaughterhouse* (1997), Gail Eisnitz investigates the beef industry and claims that cows are made to endure terrible conditions during the slaughtering process, causing them fear, dread and a painful death. In even more recent years, the beef controversies have prompted many scientists and industry experts to develop more 'humane' ways of slaughtering cows even in high-number, mechanized slaughterhouses, with well-known psychologist Grandin leading the team of research.

he issues surrounding the slaughter of cows, together other animals, are not new in concept. Religious customs nd prohibitions are probably some of the most well-known rules (in certain parts of the world) dictating the ways in which cows should be slaughtered and beef produced. In Muslim countries and culture, the slaughter of cows and the production of beef must be carried out according to allowed procedures – also known as 'halal' – as outlined by Islamic law. *Dhabiha* is the prescribed method for slaughtering animals, consisting of using a sharp knife to make a swift, deep incision in the cow's throat. The person carrying out the deed should be a Muslim of good faith and mental condition. In similar fashion, Jewish custom prescribes that cows should also

Lovis Corinth, *In the Slaughterhouse*, 1893, oil on canvas.

be slaughtered in a ritual fashion allowed by Talmudic law (also referred to as 'kosher'). The slaughtering process, known in Judaism as *shochet*, can only be performed by a trained and pious Jewish individual who strictly follows the regulations outlined by Jewish law and who has been trained to sever the carotid artery of the animal swiftly with a large sharp knife.

As both halal and kosher slaughtering methods require the cow to be conscious through the entire process and until the moment of death, the customs have caused controversies in Western countries, not only of a cultural but also a civic nature. In many areas, the practice of having the animal conscious at the point of death goes against regional and national regulations. The majority of Western countries where large Jewish and Muslim communities are present have allowed special regulations to be in place so that kosher and halal beef can be produced. This does not mean, however, that the practices are fully and widely accepted (in cultural terms) in non-Jewish and non-Muslim countries and the controversial methods have often been on the radars of humane societies and animal rights groups.

Mad Cows

In recent years, 'mad cow' disease became one of beef's most dreadful challenges. Although primarily a cattle illness, the incredibly contagious bovine spongiform encephalopathy (BSE) could be transmitted to humans through consuming parts of an infected animal, especially in the brain and digestive tracts of the carcass. In spite of the fact that the disease primarily affects the nervous system, it is also known to spread through the blood, leaving traces in the muscular tissue. Infection, therefore, could take place through consuming the flesh of cows, putting human consumers at risk. Although the disease has been known to mutate regularly and present itself through different symptoms, an illness similar to BSE – affecting mainly cattle, but known to spread to humans – was reported by Hippocrates in the fifth century BC. In the fourth century AD, Roman writer and military historian Publius Flavius Vegetius Renatus also recorded cases of the disease affecting both cattle and, on occasion, legionnaires. In its late twentieth-century incarnation, the disease affected millions of cows worldwide and virtually destroyed the cattle industry around the globe. The first reported case in North America was in 1993 and the specimens came from Alberta, Canada. The UK was famously the most affected country; the first case was diagnosed and accepted by the British Ministry of Agriculture in 1989. By 1997, more than 180,000 cattle had been diagnosed with the disease. More than four million were slaughtered and their remains destroyed as a precaution during the lengthy eradication process.

When Oprah had a Beef

In 1996 one of the biggest controversies faced by beef in the U.S. was captained by none other than Oprah Winfrey, the media mogul with an apparently enhanced social conscience. At the extreme height of the mad cow disease scare, Oprah invited Howard Lynam, a retired cattle rancher who had become vegetarian, to speak on her daytime show. The aim of the appearance was to discuss several controversial practices within the American beef industry. The most heated topic was a process – now banned in the U.S. – called 'rendering'; this involved turning cow organs into cattle feed. While Lynam's heartfelt account of the process was plagued by exaggerated statements that were challenged openly on the show, Oprah was extremely shocked by the beef industry revelations and declared that the news had stopped her 'cold from eating another hamburger'. The effect of the beef episode on the *Oprah Winfrey Show* on the cattle industry in the u.s. was devastating. Barely two weeks after the interview with Lynam had aired, beef prices plunged to a ten-year low. In response to this reaction, a group of outraged cattle ranchers from Texas filed a lawsuit – to the tune of $10 million – claiming that Oprah had slandered the entire beef industry and been responsible for its subsequent decline. A verdict was reached in Amarillo, Texas, in 1998. The cattle ranchers lost their battle, as the jury ruled in Oprah's favour. Oprah showed her happiness openly about the judgement and claimed, with a touch of irony, that she was still 'off hamburgers'.

The Beef Hormone Dispute

On an international scale, the beef hormone dispute represents another controversy – of transatlantic agricultural proportions – that has pained the cattle industry in recent times. Unsurprisingly, this controversy was also tightly connected to the era of BSE crisis, as a fear of this particular disease also raised public and scientific awareness in relation to all aspects of the beef industry. In the late 1990s, the European Union banned all meat imports that had been treated with artificial beef hormones. Beef fared particularly badly in the u.s., since artificial hormones had been used by cattle ranchers for decades. The hormones banned by the EU in cattle farming were progesterone, estradiol, testosterone, melengestrol acetate, zeranol and trenbolone acetate. While the first three

Beef disputes. Cartoonist John Jonik imagines how the cows would react to consuming their ethically disagreeable food.

are known to occur naturally in animals, the last three were artificially developed as a cost-effective way to enhance cattle growth. The EU allowed for artificial hormones to be used only as a veterinary precaution or cure and not as a growth-enhancing strategy. All meat imports that had been treated with the artificial beef hormones were banned in the EU by the end of 1996. The hormone ban, however, was met with opposition on the international market. The World Trade Organization (WTO) – while commonly using bans as part of their beef industry policies – demanded to see scientific evidence that the hormones represented a health risk to human consumers, signalling the need for a specific trade embargo. As a result of the doubts raised by the WTO – and the EU's inability to produce convincing scientific evidence – the U.S.

and Canada opposed the ban and began legal action against the EU in 1997. The clash resulted in a long battle, which ended in 1998 as the WTO found that the EU had no substantial veterinary evidence to ban the use of beef hormones. In the absence of appropriate procedures for risk assessment on the part of the EU, the ban on hormonally enhanced beef was lifted on 13 February 1998.

Organic Beef

The effect of the beef hormones dispute on consumers was great. Public awareness was raised about the possible dangers of artificially enhanced beef. As a result of the WTO's ruling in 1998, all beef is allowed on the international market – whether its growth has been enhanced with artificial hormones or not – provided it meets transcontinental quality standards. Inevitably, the thought that hormone-enhanced beef was put on the market for unaware consumers to buy generated fear and mistrust among the public. A survey conducted in the US in 2002 confirmed that more than 80 per cent of American consumers wanted to know whether the beef they were buying was treated with artificial hormones or not, demanding a label on the packet. The aftermath of the beef hormone dispute motivated American consumers to search for organically reared beef, which boosted the growth of the organic cattle industry immensely. It is estimated that between 2002 and 2003 the American organic beef industry had a growth of 77 per cent, accounting for a total profit of $23 billion within the whole organic market. In spite of the controversies, beef continues to sell. 'Organic' just functions as a new and improved label for quality that contentious American consumers strongly rely on.

hundreds of thousands of acres of tropical forest have been levelled to create pasture for cattle. Beef production is considered extremely wasteful in terms of energy and materials, since the largest amounts of corn produced around the world are actually used to feed cattle. In the U.S., half of the water consumed by the country is used to grow the corn for cattle feed. Overall, cattle farms use almost 40 per cent of the total world grain production. The beef industry has also been named as one of the main causes of desertification, as the constant pounding of hoofed cattle is said to disturb and eventually destroy the delicate roots which keep the soil layers intact.

Nonetheless, while the environment seems a far removed concern that barely touches on the cattle industry, it will not be strange to learn that health concerns for human consumers represent one of the main problems faced by contemporary beef. In nutritional terms, beef is composed mainly of protein and fat. It is also a very good source of minerals, including selenium, phosphorus, zinc and, of course, iron. Being classed as 'red meat', beef is also the principal and most significant source of carnitine, a quaternary ammonium compound that, in living organisms, is essential for the transport of fatty acids during the breakdown of lipids – a process absolutely necessary for the generation of metabolic energy. Carnitine is particularly important during growth and pregnancy, ostensibly making beef an essential part of any human's diet. With this in mind, the old mantra that 'meat is good for you' would seem to apply, with beef truly being the most apt candidate for the position. And yet recent development and research studies have endeavoured to prove otherwise.

By the end of the twentieth century beef had already been charged with several health crimes that continue to prey on the minds of aficionados of the meat today. As the twenty-first century made an appearance, beef was at centre of health controversies. Famously, a scientific connection was made between the consumption of beef and forms of human cancer. In 2007, a study released by the World Cancer Research Fund claimed there was 'strong evidence' that red meat was one of the principal causes of 'bowel cancer'. The same health report also recommended to consumers that the average consumption of beef should not exceed 300 grams per week, stating clearly that surpassing this amount corresponded to 'the level of consumption . . . at which the risk of colorectal cancer can clearly be seen to rise'.

It should not be surprising that health warnings around beef are particularly targeted at consumers in Western countries, where the consumption of fast food is statistically at its highest. A direct correlation has been established – both scientifically and in popular culture – between the consumption of fast food and the rise of health issues in the population such as diabetes and heart disease. As beef is often the meat of

Franz Marc, *Yellow Cow*, 1911, oil on canvas.

Bronze bull statue by artist Laurence Broderick, as it appears outside the avidly frequented 'Bull Ring' shopping centre in Birmingham, UK.

choice at fast food restaurants, this particular meat has been at the centre of the health controversies, since associations have been made between eating beefburgers and obesity in human beings – the ratio being particularly high in countries such as the U.S. and the UK. In the past ten years, restaurant chains such as McDonald's and Wendy's have increasingly included more 'healthy options' on their fast food menus, which do not feature beef as an ingredient at all.

However, consumed in small quantities, lean beef is indeed a great health benefit to the human body, providing minerals and protein that are essential for a healthy diet. The Harvard Public School of Health recommends small quantities of lean beef to be consumed regularly in virtue of its high selenium and vitamin B12 content. No one seems to realize that the health issues arising from consuming burgers and fast food on a regular basis do not have beef as a central factor. It is true that some beef cuts can contain high levels of saturated and (unfortunately) lean cuts of beef are seldom used by tr fast food industry, since they are expensive and require longer cooking times. What is served as the basis for beefburgers in fast food chains is often of very poor quality and, in several instances, mixed with fat and connective tissue to increase its bulk. In addition, most regular consumers of fast food greatly exceed the recommended dose of this particular type of food, getting through enormous quantities of cheap beefburgers. Human greed and fattening cooking methods – often rich in oil and butter-based sauces – have indeed shaped the quality of the eating experience in fast food chains and, in so doing, have ruined the reputation of beef in the minds of thousands of consumers around the world.

Epilogue:
A Beefy Afterthought

Controversially or not, beef continues to have a hold on the world's culinary preferences, economies and cultures. It seems odd to listen to the various claims that deem beef and the cattle industry as the primary agents in the degradation of many developed and Westernized countries. Although one cannot deny that the impact of the burger almost transcends issues of mere hunger in contemporary cultures, it is strange to think of beef as the main culprit in the destruction of human society and health. Beef has existed in human societies for thousands of years, long before capitalism and consumerism had made their appearances, some say as plagues of human existence.

In spite of the problems surrounding the cattle industry, it would definitely be unwise to end an assessment of beef's history on a negative note. Beef gives us an insight into a culture's ways of life; methods of preparation, eating customs and perceived prized cuts offer us a hands-on interpretation of what human groups favour and dislike on both local and global scales. Beef is entangled with so many layers of social life that its presence on family and restaurant menus signals the attachment to a sense of tradition and custom which often forms the basis for imagined systems of belief and organization.

Beef refuses to disappear from our tables and our industries. Its ability to generate controversy is itself revealing of the inquisitive wonder that is the human mind. If it is true that human societies developed alongside beef, then we must pay attention to how we produce this meat. Beef is not just a way to feed: it is a reflection of our customs, beliefs and values.

Recipes

Historic Recipes

For the modern cook, making beef recipes from earlier times can be a frustrating experience. In historical cookbooks very little attention is dedicated to measurements and timings. Assembling the right ingredients can also be an exasperating task, since – in most documented cases – it was common practice to amalgamate the necessary ingredients into the basic instructions, rather than having them clearly listed. Nonetheless, beef's innate versatility allows an inventive and adventurous modern cook to add a little touch of personalization to the historical recipe, without sacrificing any of the taste and purpose that were wholeheartedly intended by the bygone chefs.

Bubula Fricta
—from *Apicius de re Coquinaria* (*c.* AD 940); this translation is based chiefly on Albanus Torinus' Latin edition (1541)

For a sauce with fried beef take pepper, lovage, celery seed, cumin, origanum, dry onions, raisins, honey, vinegar, wine, broth, oil and reduced must.

NOTE: Some of the ingredients for *Bubula Fricta* – especially the 'reduced must' – might be difficult to locate in our modern kitchens.

If you cannot find reduced must, a splash of reduced red wine will do the trick. The taste might not be as 'authentic' as intended, but it will still be an excellent rendition of an ancient Roman recipe.

Boiled Beef and Leeks
—from anon., *Bald's Leechbook II* (*c.* AD 950)

Against hiccupy stomachs or swellings take [horned cattle] flesh [seethed/boiled/cooked] in vinegar and with oil [thickened] with salt and dill and leek, partake of that [for] a seven night, henceforth relieven thence the afflicted stomach.

Stewed Broathe for Bief
—from anon., *A Propre New Booke for Cokery* (*c.* 1545)

Take halfe a handful of rosemary and as muche of tyme / and bynder it on a bundell with threde after it is washen / and put it in the pot / after that the pot is clene skyned / and lette it boilc a while / then cur soppes of white bread and put them in a great charger and put on the same skaldynge broth / and whan it is soken ynough / strayne it through a strainer with a quantitie of wyne or good Ale / so that it be not to tarte / and when it is strainer / poure it in a pot and than put in your raysons and prunes and so let them boyle tyl the meate is inough. If the broathe to be sweete/ put in the more wyne / orels a lytell vinegar.

Collar'd Beef
—from Hannah Woolley, *The Queen-like Closet* (1672)

Take a good Flank of Beef, and lay it in Pump water and Salt, or rather Saltpeter, one day and one night, then take Pepper, Mace, Nutmegs, Ginger, and Cloves, with a little of the Herb called Tarragon, beat your Spice, shred your Tarragon, and mingle these with some Suet beaten small, and strew upon your Beef, and so rowl it up, and tie it hard, and bake it in a pot with Claret Wine and Butter, let the pot be covered close, and something – in the pot to keep the Meat down in the Liquor that it may not scorch, set it into the Oven with Houshold bread, and when it is baked, take it out, and let it cool, then hang it up one night in the Chimney before you eat it, and so as long as you please.

NOTE: Some of us may not have a 'chimney' ready to accommodate our newly prepared beef dishes. If this applies to you, covering the dish with foil (for a short while) or storing it in an airtight container (for a longer period of time) will work perfectly.

Beef Royal

—from Hannah Glasse, *The Art of Cookery Made Plain and Easy* (1747)

Take a sirloin of beef, or a large rump, bone it and beat it very well, then lard it with bacon, season it all over, with salt, pepper, mace, cloves and nutmeg, all beat fine, some lemon-peel cut small, and some sweet herbs; in the meantime make a strong broth of the bone; take a piece of butter with a little flour, brown it, put in the beef; keep it turning often till it is brown, then strain the broth, put all together into a pot, put in a bay leaf, a few truffles, and some ox palates cut small; cover it close, and let it stew till it is tender; take out the beef, skim off all the fat, pour in a pint of claret, some fried oysters, an anchovy, and some gerkins shred small; boil all together, put in the beef to warm, thicken your sauce with a piece of butter rolled in flour, or mushroom powder. Lay your meat in the dish, pour the sauce over it, and send it to the table. This may be eaten either hot or cold.

Olives of Beef
—from Elizabeth Moxon, *English Housewifry* (1764)

Take some slices of a rump (or any other tender piece) of beef, and beat them with a paste pin, season them with nutmeg, pepper and salt, and rub them over with the yolk of an egg; make a little forc'd-meat of veal, beef-suet, a few bread crumbs, sweet-herbs, a little shred mace, pepper, salt, and two eggs, mixed all together; take two or three slices of the beef, according as they are in bigness, and a lump of forc'd-meat the size of an egg; lay your beef round it, and roll it in part of a kell of veal, put it into an earthen dish, with a little water, a glass of claret, and a little onion shred small; lay upon them a little butter, and bake them in an oven about an hour; when they come out take off the fat, and thicken the gravy with a little butter and flour; six of them is enough for a side dish. Garnish the dish with horseradish and pickles.

To Make Beef Tea
—from William Kitchiner, *Apicius Redivivus; Or, The Cook's Oracle* (1817)

Cut a pound of lean gravy meat into thin slices; put it into a quart and half a pint of cold water; set it over a very gentle fire, where it will become gradually warm; when the scum rises, let it continue simmering gently for about an hour; then strain it through a fine sieve or a napkin; let it stand ten minutes to settle, and then pour off the clear tea.

Boiled Beef
—from Charles Elmé Francatelli, *A Plain Cookery Book for the Working Classes* (1852)

This is an economical dinner, especially where there are many mouths to feed. Buy a few pounds of either salt brisket, thick or thin flank, or buttock of beef; these pieces are always to be had at a low rate. Let us suppose you have bought a piece of salt beef for a Sunday's dinner, weighing about five pounds, at 6½d. per pound, that would come to 2s. 8½d.; two pounds of common flour, 4d., to be made into suet pudding or dumplings, and say 8½d. for cabbages, parsnips, and potatoes; altogether 3s. 9d. This would produce a substantial dinner for ten persons in family, and would, moreover, as children do not require much meat when they have pudding, admit of there being enough left to help out the next day's dinner, with potatoes.

Beef Collops
—from Isabella Beeton, *Mrs Beeton's Book of Household Management* (1861)

Mode: Have the steak cut thin, and divide it in pieces about 3 inches long; beat these with the blade of a knife, and dredge with flour. Put them in a frying pan with the butter, and let them fry for about 3 minutes; then lay them in a small stewpan, and pour over them the gravy. Add a piece of butter, kneaded with a little flour, put in the seasoning and all the other ingredients, and let the whole simmer, but not boil, for 10 minutes. Serve in a hot covered dish.

Frizzled Beef
—from F. L. Gillette, *The Whitehouse Cookbook* (1887)

Shave off *very thin* slices of smoked or dried beef, put them in a frying pan, cover with cold water, set it on the back of the range or stove, and let it come to a very slow heat, allowing it time to swell out to its natural size, but not to boil. Stir it up, then drain off the water. Melt one ounce of sweet butter in the frying pan and add the wafers of beef. When they begin to frizzle or turn up, break over them three eggs; stir until the eggs are cooked; add a little white pepper, and serve on slices of buttered toast.

Beef Stew

—from C. Houston Goudiss and Alberta M. Goudiss, *Foods That Will Win The War And How To Cook Them* (1918)

Soak one-half of the meat [450 g/1 lb of meat from the neck, cross ribs, shin or knuckles] cut in small pieces, in the quart of water for one hour. Heat slowly to boiling point. Season the other half of the meat with salt and pepper. Roll in flour. Brown in three table-spoons of fat with the onion. Add to the soaked meat, which has been brought to the boiling point. Cook for one hour or until tender. Add the vegetables, and flour mixed with half cup of cold water. Cook until vegetables are tender.

Chili of Beef

—from Mary Wilson, *Mrs Wilson's Cook Book* (1920)

Cut flank steak in one-inch blocks and then roll in flour and brown quickly in hot fat. Add onions, pimentoes, tomatoes and water. Cook slowly until meat is tender and then season with salt and paprika. Add beans. Heat to boiling point and then serve.

Modern Recipes

Eye Fillet with Warm Potato Salad

—Ray McVinnie, professional chef, food editor, columnist and judge
on *MasterChef New Zealand*. Printed with permission.

This recipe makes a simple but tasty dish suitable either for an everyday family dinner or as part of a special multi-course meal.

800 g (1 lb 12 oz) eye fillet of beef in one piece, trimmed of all
fat and sinew
30 ml (2 tablespoons) olive oil
½ teaspoon coarsely ground black pepper
800 g (1 lb 12 oz) new potatoes, well scrubbed
2 spring onions, thinly sliced
3 tablespoons capers
zest and juice of 1 lemon
extra virgin olive oil

Preheat the oven to 200°C/400°F. Rub the oil and pepper all over the beef. Heat an ovenproof frying pan over a high heat and brown the beef all over. Place the pan in the oven for about 10 minutes to cook medium rare. Turn the beef once or twice as it cooks. Remove from the oven and rest in a warm place for 5 minutes. Meanwhile boil the potatoes in plenty of well-salted water until tender. Drain well and slice. Place on a serving platter and sprinkle the spring onions, capers and lemon zest on top. Dribble plenty of extra virgin olive oil and lemon juice over everything. Season with salt and pepper. Slice the beef thinly, place on top of the potatoes and serve with salsa spooned over the top.

Serves 4–6

Monkey-gland Steak

3 medium onions, peeled and coarsely chopped
15 ml (1 tablespoon) cooking oil
30 ml (2 tablespoons) tomato sauce
30 ml (2 tablespoons) Worcestershire sauce
30 ml (2 tablespoons) vinegar
500 g (1 lb) steak, such as rump steak
salt and pepper

Sauté the onions in the cooking oil until light brown. Add the tomato sauce, Worcestershire sauce and vinegar. Season with salt and pepper and simmer for about 2 minutes, stirring continuously. Cut the meat into portions. Season with salt and pepper. Place the steak in the sauce mixture and fry on both sides over a moderate heat until done, taking care not to burn the meat. Serve hot with mashed potatoes, peas and salad.

NOTE: Needless to say, 'monkey-gland' steak has nothing to do with monkeys. The origin of the dish is shrouded in mystery. One likely explanation, however, sees some French chefs lured to work at the old Carlton Hotel in Johannesburg in the early 1950s. The story claims that the patrons of the hotel lacked the sophistication to appreciate the many fine nuances of haute cuisine, especially when it came to meat. Exasperated by the diners' requests for well done steaks, the chefs concocted a sauce made with what they saw as the most commercial and least refined ingredients they could find in their kitchen. Pleased with the result, they proclaimed it to be 'monkey-gland sauce', which they smothered generously on newly grilled steaks. The chefs' joke proved popular with the clientele's taste buds and, just like that, a South African culinary legend was born.

Modern Beef Bulgogi

—Michael Choi, Professional Chef (School of Hospitality and Tourism, Auckland University of Technology)

This dish is a reinvention of traditional Korean *bulgogi* dish with accompaniments.

Bul go gi Steak Marinade
300 g (10 oz) eye fillet
90 ml (6 tablespoons) soy sauce
90 ml (6 tablespoons) water
45 g (1½ oz) sugar
20 ml (1 tablespoon) sesame oil
15 g (½ oz) garlic, minced
15 g (½ oz) spring onion, finely chopped
pinch of ground black pepper

Mix ingredients well and marinate the beef in them overnight. Pre-heat the oven to 200°C/400°F. Grill or pan-sear the beef on a hot pan and then roast in the oven for 5–6 minutes (medium rare). Let the meat rest for 5 minutes and slice into 6 pieces.

Crispy Oxtail Roll
bul go gi marinade
1 kg (2 lb 2 oz) oxtail
100 g (3½ oz) carrot, cut into 5–6 pieces
200 g (7 oz) onion, chopped
1 spring roll sheet

Use *bulgogi* marinade to marinate oxtail overnight. Cook in a pressure cooker for 45–60 minutes. Remove the meat from the bones while still warm. Roll onto the spring roll sheet 10 cm (4 inch) long and 1 cm (½ inch) thick. Panfry until golden.

Sesame Rice Ball
100 g (3½ oz) cooked rice (short grain)
20 g (½ oz) toasted sesame seeds

Roll the rice into 4 balls and coat with sesame seeds. Garnish with cherry tomatoes, asparagus spears (blanched), one courgette (sliced lengthwise and blanched), *enoki* mushrooms, watercress and shallots.

Serves 2

Mamma Elena's Traditional Beef Carpaccio

500 g (1 lb) beef fillet
juice of 2 lemons
rocket
olive oil to taste
Grana Padano cheese to taste
100 g (3½ oz) rocket
salt and pepper

Cut the raw beef fillet into thin slices. Portion slices into individual plates. Squeeze some lemon juice onto each slice. Top each plate with rocket, olive oil and Grana Padano shavings. Season with salt and pepper and enjoy.

Serves 4–6

Modern Sukiyaki
—John Kelleher, Professional Chef (School of Hospitality and Tourism, Auckland University of Technology)

This is a plated version of the classic Japanese one-pot dish, now a delicacy in Japan due to the high price of grain-fed beef.

15 g (1 tablespoon) grapeseed oil
200 g (7 oz) beef sirloin, well marbled
3–4 baby leeks or spring onions, cut on the bias
200 g (7 oz) *ito konnyaku* noodles or *shirataki*

1 large Portobello mushroom, cut into 6 pieces
½ grilled tofu (*yakidōfu*) cake
handful of baby mizuna or rocket

Sauce
75 g (5 tablespoons) mirin
75 g (5 tablespoons) sake
75 g (5 tablespoons) dark soy sauce
30 g (2 tablespoons) palm sugar
100 g (3½ oz) *dashi*, prepared (Japanese stock)
2 eggs, lightly beaten (optional)

Massage the oil onto the sirloin then season with sea salt and freshly milled black pepper.

Prepare the sauce by bringing to the boil the mirin and saké. Add the soy sauce, sugar and *dashi* and reduce the heat to medium, simmer uncovered. Grill the 2-cm (¾-inch) thick piece of beef on a hot griddle pan until evenly marked with a criss-cross design, and add to the simmering sauce – remove from the broth when medium cooked, don't overcook, keep warm. Lightly grill the seasoned baby leeks, set aside. Meanwhile, rinse the *ito konnyaku* in warm water for one minute until the noodles become whiter, drain and set aside. Add the mushroom, tofu and grilled baby leeks to the sauce to finish the cooking process. Finally, add the noodles.

To serve, remove the noodles and place on a hot plate to resemble a flowing river, arrange the rest of the hot ingredients along the noodles. Garnish with baby *mizuna* leaves. Serve with steamed white rice and try dipping a slice of beef in the beaten egg.

Serves 2

Select Bibliography

Applestone, Joshua and Jessica, *The Butcher's Guide to Well-raised Meat* (London, 2011)

Byard, Jack, *Know Your Cattle* (London, 2008)

Civitello, Linda, *Cuisine and Culture: A History of Food and People* (Oxford, 2009)

Clutton-Brock, Juliet, *A Natural History of Domesticated Mammals* (London, 1999)

Davidson, Alan, *The Oxford Companion to Food* (Oxford, 1999)

Fiddes, Nick, *Meat: A Natural Symbol* (London, 1991)

Fussell, Betty, *Raising Steaks: The Life and Times of American Beef* (Boston, MA, 1999)

Grandin, Temple, *Humane Livestock Handling: Understanding Livestock Behaviour and Building Facilities for Healthier Farms* (North Adams, MA, 2008)

Hunt, Tamara, *Defining John Bull: Political Caricature and National Identity in Late Georgian England* (Farnham, 2003)

Kiple, Kenneth F., and Kremhild Coneé Ornelas, *The Cambridge World History of Food*, vols I and II (Cambridge and New York, 2001)

Mariani, John F., *The Encyclopedia of American Food and Drink* (New York, 1999)

Mennell, Stephen, *All Manners of Food: Eating and Taste in England and France from the Middle Ages to the Present* (Urbana, IL, 1995)

Montgomery, M. R., *A Cow's Life: The Surprising History of Cattle*

and How the Black Angus Came to be Home on the Range
(New York, 2004)

Murray, Sarah, *Moveable Feasts; From Ancient Rome to the 21st Century,
the Incredible Journeys of the Foods We Eat* (New York, 2007)

Ozersky, Josh, *Hamburger: A History* (New Haven, CT, 2008)

Piatti-Farnell, Lorna, *Food and Culture in Contemporary American
Fiction* (New York, 2011)

Rhulman, Michael, Brian Polcyn and Thomas Keller, *Charcuterie:
The Craft of Salting, Smoking and Curing* (New York, 2005)

Rifkin, Jeremy, *Beyond Beef: The Rise and Fall of Cattle Culture*
(New York, 1993)

Rimas, Andrew, and Evan Fraser, *Beef: The Untold Story of How
Milk, Meat and Muscle Shaped the World* (New York, 2009)

Robbins, Richard, *Global Problems and the Culture of Capitalism*
(London, 2010)

Rogers, Ben, *Beef and Liberty: Roast Beef, John Bull and the English
Nation* (London, 2003)

Schlosser, Eric, *Fast Food Nation: What the All-American Meal is
Doing to the World* (London, 2002)

Shiva, Vandana, *Stolen Harvest: The Hijacking of the Global Food
Supply* (Cambridge, MA, 2000)

Sim, Alison, *Food and Feast in Tudor England* (London, 2005)

Smith, Andrew F., *Hamburger: A Global History* (London, 2008)

Standage, Tom, *An Edible History of Humanity* (New York, 2010)

Tannahill, Reay, *Food in History* (London, 1988)

Thomas, Keith, *Man and the Natural World: Changing Attitudes in
England, 1500–1800* (London, 1983)

Torode, John, *Beef and Other Bovine Matters* (Newton, CT, 2009)

Toussaint-Samat, Maguelonne, *A History of Food* (Oxford, 2000)

Velten, Hannah, *Cow* (London, 2007)

Websites and Associations

American Angus Association
www.angus.org

Argentine Beef Association
www.argentinebeef.org.ar

British Agricultural History Society
www.bahs.org.uk

Gode Cookery
www.godecookery.com

Historic Food
www.historicfood.com

Kobe Beef America
www.kobe-beef.com

New Zealand Beef Association
www.beef.org.nz

The Bovine Bazaar
www.bovinebazaar.com

The Food Timeline
www.foodtimeline.org

u.s. Department of Agriculture
www.usda.gov

Acknowledgements

Writing this book was a very different experience for me and I absolutely loved it. I am very grateful to Andrew F. Smith, editor of the Edible Series, and Michael Leaman at Reaktion Books for giving me the opportunity to delve into the history of beef.

I am grateful to Ray McVinnie, Michael Choi and John Kelleher from the School of Hospitality and Tourism (Auckland University of Technology) for showing so much interest in the project and contributing their beef recipes and photographs.

Thanks go to Catherine Orr and Colette Wood for their help with South African beef recipes and preparation methods. I am grateful to Marjory Farnell for discussing historical recipes with me at length, and Alessandra Mastrogiacomo for providing photographs of the traditional bresaola. Very special thanks go to Frances Nelson, for sharing her culinary memories of hot summer days in New Zealand.

I am incredibly grateful to all my friends and family for their endless help and support. A special 'thank you' goes to my mamma and papá, Elena e Giorgio, who were incredibly patient and listened to me dutifully, while I spent hours talking about beef.

Finally, and as always, my most heartfelt thanks go to my husband, Rob Farnell, who never doubts me.

Photo Acknowledgements

The author and the publishers wish to express their thanks to the below sources of illustrative material and/or permission to reproduce it:

Author's collection: pp. 23, 56, 74, 79, 100, 101, 106; Deitchman/ McNeill: p. 8; Charles Hamilton Smith: p. 9; The Louvre: pp. 12, 16, 94; Metropolitan Museum of Art / Rama: p. 13; British Museum: p. 18; Shadwell Aberdeen Angus/ Justin Eric: p. 15; Art City LV: p. 25; John Oxley Library, Queensland: p. 31; Biblioteca Casanatense, Rome: p. 39; Adactio: p. 43; Michael Choi: p. 40, Mjoro: p. 46; Rainer Zenz: p. 64; The British World: p. 70; Eigene Autnahme: p. 6), Sebastian von Kracht: p. 75; Ivan: p. 87; Minneapolis Institute of Arts: p. 90; Archie MacDonald: p. 83; FoodieBuddha: p. 81; Sifu Renka: p. 87; Orlando Calvo: p. 28; Tate Britain: p. 96; Metro Goldwyn Meyer: p. 102; Shutterstock: p. 105; Staatsgalerie Stuttgart: p. 110; Cushing Memorial Library: p. 109; John Jonik: p. 114; sdadefend.com; p. 116; Luke Byfield: p. 120; Guggenheim Museum, New York: p. 119.

Index

italic numbers refer to illustrations; **bold** to recipes